D1601481

Fascism

Issues in Contemporary Civilization

Fascism	Renzo De Felice
Genocide	Irving Louis Horowitz
Socialism	Seymour Martin Lipset
Détente	Aleksandr Solzhenitsyn

TRANSACTION ISSUES

IN CONTEMPORARY CIVILIZATION

Fascism

An Informal Introduction to Its Theory and Practice

Renzo De Felice

An interview with
Michael A. Ledeen

Transaction Books
New Brunswick, New Jersey

Library of Congress Catalog Number: 76-13006.
ISBN: 0-87855-190-5 (cloth) 0-87855-619-2 (paper).

First Italian-language edition, *Intervista sul fascismo*,
Gius. Laterza and Figli, 1975.

Library of Congress Cataloging in Publication Data
Felice, Renzo De.
   Fascism: an informal introduction to its theory and practice.
   (Issues in Contemporary Civilization)
   Translation of Intervista sul fascismo.
   Bibliography: p.
   1. Fascism. 2. Fascism—Italy. I. Ledeen, Michael Arthur,
1941-   joint author. II. Title.
JC481.F36513   320.5'33   76-13006
ISBN 0-87855-190-5
      0-87855-619-2

Contents

Introduction

This book originally appeared in Italy at the beginning of July 1975 entitled: *Intervista sul fascismo*. By the middle of the month it was the best-selling paperback in the country, and at this writing (mid-October) it is still number one on the best-seller list. It has sold over fifty thousand copies (a remarkable figure in a country with a population of sixty million, an illiteracy rate of over thirty percent, and where only one person out of ten reads a daily newspaper). It has been the object of long diatribes from several of the country's leading intellectuals, and the subject of front-page editorials in the official newspapers of both the Communist and Neofascist parties. It has twice been the subject of primetime programs on the national television network. Renzo De Felice has been called everything from "soft on Mussolini" to "depraved," and has been accused of trying to "rehabilitate fascism." In short, it is the most controversial book of the year in a highly charged political atmosphere.

It will not be immediately obvious to the American reader that this short volume warrants such an emotional reaction. Fascism is not nearly as important an issue to us as it is for Italians, and the American intellectual world is not, happily, as sharply divided along ideological lines. For Italian intellectuals, the terms *fascist* and *antifascist* continue to be the hard currency of contemporary political debate (one might almost say that if you are not one, you are automatically the other in the present Italian atmosphere). When De Felice suggests that fascism describes a moment in the Italian past—and only that—he is challenging the very heart of current orthodoxy. The nature of his analysis of the recent Italian past is itself at odds with the traditional version, and represents a radical departure from conventional wisdom.

De Felice's ideas about fascism have a broad significance, quite apart from their importance in the contemporary Italian scene. Perhaps no one knows as much about fascism, and no one has given the subject such rigorous historical analysis (his biography of Mussolini has progressed to 1936 in four long tomes, and will eventually run to some five thousand pages). In the course of our discussion, De Felice observed that he had been the first to consult the documents of the Fascist Regime, and had consequently had a distinct advantage over every other analyst: He alone was able to base his studies on a careful scrutiny of Fascist records. This in itself would have been sufficient to guarantee his importance in the scholarly community, but as his work continued, De Felice discovered that there were vast quantities of documentation that had not been turned over to the state, and remained in private hands. It is a tribute to the objectivity of his work that many of those people who held these documents came forward with them. De Felice therefore based his work on the most thorough documentation possible. As a by-product of his research, Renzo De Felice has today an important archive, and anyone wishing to research the fascist period must touch base with him. Happily, he is not jealous of his private collection, and dozens of volumes on fascism—written by both Italians and foreigners—have been made possible by De Felice's help and encouragement.

Given his preeminence, one is inevitably driven to wonder why he has been so intensely attacked in Italy. He is Italy's best-known historian of the contemporary period. He commands international esteem. Yet Italians give him far less credit than non-Italians. In order to understand the controversial nature of De Felice's work, we must first look at his analysis of fascism.

FASCISM RECONSIDERED

Fascism has been variously interpreted during the course of the past half century, and we are far from arriving at a consensus. Roughly speaking, there are two broad groupings of students of the fascist phenomenon: Those who embrace an external explanation, and those who believe that one must study it from within. The first group propounds that fascism was a means of manipulating the masses, and that its content was inconsequential. The second group believes that fascism was in part a mass movement, and that one must examine the beliefs of the fascists in order to understand its success. In the first group one finds the Marxists and the cynics, like, for example, A. J. P. Taylor:

> Everything about Fascism was a fraud. The social peril from which it saved Italy was a fraud; the revolution by which it seized power was a fraud; the ability and policy of Mussolini was [sic] fraudulent. Fascist rule was cor-

rupt, incompetent, empty; Mussolini himself was a vain, blundering boaster without either ideas or aims.[1]

This view of fascism is common to many scholars who seek the explanation for fascist successes either in techniques of mass manipulation or in the mechanism of repression. Marxists, for example, view fascism as the reaction of industrialists and large landowners to the threat of a socialist revolution, and as the means by which the ruling class of capitalism crushed revolutionary forces and kept them in check for twenty years. The content of fascism is beside the point to such an analysis, for whatever fascists themselves might have had to say about their intentions, their actual historical role was to bring about the triumph of the counterrevolution.

Many Western political scientists adopted this external perspective. Some distinguished students of mass movements, such as Hannah Arendt, Carl J. Friedrich, and Zbigniew Brzezinski, have viewed fascism as a form of mass control unique to the twentieth century—a form of totalitarianism—that embraces not only Italian and German fascisms but also Stalinist Russia and perhaps some other dictatorships as well (Perónist Argentina, Communist China, and so on). This model helps to put the form of fascist government in broader perspective, but it ignores the content of fascist ideology, and reduces it to a mere technique of power. By concentrating on the techniques and institutions of totalitarianism, these analysts frequently obscured profound national differences among the various regimes, and left the question of their origins and internal characteristics largely unexamined.

In recent years some scholars have preferred an internal explanation of fascism, attempting to analyze its success in each separate country rather than searching for a general model. They have tried to explain fascist triumphs in terms of emotional appeal, effective programs, charisma of fascist leaders, and use of repression. While most everyone who studies fascism believes in the class-bound nature of its origins, the new generation of analysts has insisted that fascism became a national phenomenon and eventually embraced all classes in its mantle. This latter development calls for clarification, and cannot be explained away by continuing to call fascism a counterrevolutionary regime. Many workers were recruited to the fascist cause, and little in the way of effective antifascism emerged from the proletariat (or anywhere else) before the bankruptcy of fascist foreign policy became evident. If one tries to explain fascism's success in coopting the masses in terms of mere techniques of manipulation, one is left with a dismal theory of human nature: Man is readily duped by his leaders. Many scholars prefer to look for fascism's success in the minds of its supporters, and have found that there was indeed a basis for its mass appeal.[2]

De Felice's work on fascism is one of the most important contributions to an internal understanding of Mussolini's Italy. His mammoth biography of the Duce has revealed a remarkably talented demagogue who, for all his many insights into Italian character and his mastery of the Italian masses, never possessed sufficient coherence of vision to establish a viable basis for a fascist regime. Despite the many accusations of sympathy for his subject that have been directed against De Felice, Mussolini has emerged from the four volumes published to date as a profound failure. He never managed to create a new ruling class for his country, never had enough confidence in

the Italian people to permit them a genuine participation in fascism, and wasted his time in a constant,
almost paranoid surveillance of every detail of daily
events. Nonetheless, Mussolini remained in power
for over twenty years, while very few Italian governments in this century have managed anything re-
motely resembling that tenure. De Felice has attempted to understand fascism's durability in terms
of a political consensus, fragile to be sure, but no less
real for its feebleness. The nature of this consensus
lies at the heart of the debate over De Felice's interpretation of fascism.

There has long been a general agreement among
scholars that Italian fascism represented a sort of
pretorian guard for Italian industry and organized
agriculture against the menace of revolutionary
forces. Those people who joined Fascist squads and
fought the Socialists in the streets of Italy from 1920
onward have been viewed as members of the lower-
middle class, who fought the leftists because they
were afraid of being proletarianized. Trapped in a
desperate economic situation, menaced by loss of
property and status by the postwar crisis and by en-
swampment from below by the Socialists, these
members of the petite bourgeoisie are said to have
provided the muscle for fascism's street fights against
their class enemies. Advocates of this theory insist
that these elements were threatened with pro-
letarianization, and that this menace accounts for the
counterrevolutionary aspect of early fascism. De
Felice does not view the matter exclusively in this
light, suggesting that there was a sizable element
within Fascist ranks that was not threatened at all,
but was rising. In his view there was a revolutionary
element within fascism that embodied the desires of
emerging sectors of the middle class seeking to assert

themselves. If De Felice is correct about this—there is a growing body of sociological data that suggests that he is—conventional wisdom will have to be abandoned.

This theory has important consequences. If emerging sectors of the middle class were crucial in the formation of the Fascist movement, it would help explain a certain radical element present within fascism throughout its life span. There were always those people who believed that fascism was revolutionary—indeed, the only truly revolutionary phenomenon in the country. These fascist "revolutionaries" believed that fascism would eventually transform Italians, Italy, and the entire West. They continued to believe this for quite a long time, until the reactionary nature of Mussolini's regime became so plain that even they had to recognize it. But from the march on Rome until the Spanish civil war, many fascists believed they were participants in a revolution (and that they would play a major role in the new society of the future). De Felice calls this the "Fascist movement," and it was a constant thorn in Mussolini's side. In the end, many of those who participated in the Fascist movement opposed Mussolini and the regime, believing they had been betrayed. Many joined the ranks of antifascism and then of the Resistance. Others remained loyal to Mussolini, embracing fascist anti-Semitism in a last desperate attempt to transform fascism.

The Fascist movement was part of the fascist consensus, but by no means the most numerous. The consensus of which De Felice has written, which extended roughly from the concordat to the Ethiopian war, was primarily based on a popular view of Mussolini's government as having protected Italy from many of the ills that beset Western Europe: The threat of war, a grave economic crisis, and social violence and instability. Fascism was valued not so much for what it had given Italy, but for the perils it had avoided. This was no small feat in a period that saw government after government fall in Western Europe, and the United States plunged into the Great Depression.

Here again De Felice is at odds with most scholars of fascism, who have viewed Mussolini's mass support as based on a spurious appeal to Italian grandeur and military prowess. De Felice claims, for example, that Italians were exceedingly concerned about the outbreak of the Ethiopian war, fearing that England and France might decide to oppose Italian colonialization of Ethiopia and thus involve their country in war. This is a far cry from the traditional view of Mussolini orchestrating a frenzy of imperialistic fervor prior to the invasion, and it suggests that Italians were not quite so easily manipulated as has been previously maintained. Fascist consensus was quite fragile, especially considering the growing desire of the regime to demonstrate Italy's might on the world stage. De Felice claims (although as yet his analysis has not been published) that consensus was fractured at the moment when fascism took on an explicitly imperialistic stance, joined with Hitler, and entered the Spanish civil war.

One might expect De Felice to argue that Italy's entry into World War II was not popular with the people, but the reverse is true. He paints a picture of Mussolini as indecisive, wondering when to enter, and even which side to join! The fact of primary importance, according to De Felice, was that once the fall of France was assured, Mussolini felt further delay might risk long-term reprisals from the

Führer, and at the same time Italian public opinion swung sharply behind entry into the war alongside the victorious Germans. One is forced to rethink old "truths": The Axis turns out to have been not an ideological alliance between two fascist dictators but a tactical decision based on both foreign and domestic considerations. According to De Felice, there were profound differences between fascism and nazism; so much so as to raise serious doubts about the utility of applying the term *fascist* to both.

With this claim, De Felice challenged not only a commonplace of Italian historiography, but an important political tradition as well. The Italian Resistance was waged more against nazi forces than against Italian fascist ones, and political rhetoric has labeled this struggle one against "nazifascism." Such concepts are not easily abandoned, and no single claim of De Felice's has caused so much turmoil as this. Yet here De Felice is at one with a large body of literature in the United States, France, and Germany, which has taken great pains to distinguish between the two regimes.

As if to rub salt into the wounds of his critics, De Felice claims that the Fascist movement was linked, albeit spuriously, to a Western radical tradition going back to the days of the Terror in the French Revolution. Fascism, he argues, contains both a well-defined theory of human progress and a conception of the popular will that ties it to the extremist Rousseauian themes of the Terror and the "totalitarian democracy" that it spawned. For those who viewed fascism as the archetype of a reactionary system of government, this was too much to stomach, and it was called "an affront to common sense" by some critics. Yet most scholars of fascism would agree

with this claim, and the most recent textbook on
fascism in the United States makes the very same
statement.[3]

This book was quite controversial (and deliberately
so) within the context of the Italian historiographical
and political traditions. The intensity of the response
was so great that one must consider yet another of De
Felice's provocative claims: That fascism left antifascists with a certain intolerant mentality as part of its
heritage.

THE STORM OVER DE FELICE

Attacks against De Felice started even before the
book was published, when the publishing house gave
galleys of the text to the editors of Italy's most widely
read weekly magazine, *l'Espresso*. The theses of the
book were immediately distorted ("was that Mussolini over there a bit left-wing?"), and Giuliano Pro-
cacci, a leading communist historian, claimed that
antifascist attitudes were absolutely necessary for an
understanding of fascism. This was demonstrated, he
said, by the fact that the first serious analyses of
fascism came from Marxists, and even those (few)
non-Marxists who wrote well on the subject had been
opponents of the regime (such as Don Sturzo).

Leaving aside for the moment the embarrassing
detail that most fascist intellectuals started out as
Marxists, this "objection" (which was a common one)
stems from the very core of Italian intellectual tradition. Italian intellectuals (like many French and
German scholars) believe that scholarship is not simply an empirical exercise in organizing data in a
coherent way, but rather must be based on an already
elaborated ideology. A proper world view—whether
it be Marxism, Freudianism, Catholicism, or

whatever—is not only essential for understanding the past, but also for present and future actions. Analysis of the past is thus ineluctably tied to present activity. For Marxist intellectuals—and the majority of contemporary Italian intellectuals seem to be Marxists—a proper world view involves the conviction the fascism was the product of a class struggle between the proletariat on the one hand, and agrarian and industrial classes on the other. There is also the conviction that everything about fascism was (and is) evil, to be condemned and rejected and fought on all fronts. In a certain sense, further research on the subject was redundant, since the conclusions were already known.

From this point of view it was clear that De Felice must have had some Machiavellian motives for his writing, and in short order various critics attempted to identify them. A young Marxist, Nicola Tranfaglia, wrote: "Italian and international circumstances which need not be recalled here . . . have reignited, in a manner one would not have believed a few years ago, the debate . . . on the Fascist phenomenon."[4] With this ominous beginning, Tranfaglia went on to suggest that De Felice's ideas might cause grave damage among the young and uninitiated, and that De Felice had undertaken "a rehabilitation of Fascism." Tranfaglia said that all serious work in the field showed how nonsensical De Felice's arguments were, and he closed by asking rhetorically whether it was productive to reopen discussion on points that had already been fully resolved, "unless, to be sure, the entire operation is purely political, and has very little to do with historiography."[5]

This was paradigmatic of many attacks against the book. Since "everybody knew" the correct interpretation, why was De Felice challenging it? The "only" explanation was that he was attempting a political maneuver, designed to undermine the forces of antifascism (in Italy today, political rhetoric has divided the world into two groups: fascists and antifascists). There was no such thing as pure scholarship. A later attack by another radical intellectual made this clear: "If one believes that being an 'objective' historian of fascism today in Italy means ... undertaking a dispassionate intellectual adventure, one may also believe that writing history is only an elegant academic profession. But it is not."[6]

What is it then? It is a "polemical" activity, according to Giovanni Ferrara, author of these lines. He suggested that De Felice was rather perverse. Had he not spent hours and months interviewing squalid individuals to discover "something which, all in all, one could have discovered without so much discomfort, namely, that 'they, too, are men'"?[7] For Ferrara, De Felice was to be held responsible for the fact that there was no good analysis of Italian antifascism. Calling De Felice's work a kind of historiographic monument to fascism, he closed his case.

There was a good deal more of this sort of attack, designed to discredit De Felice without ever really grappling with his theses. It is one thing to condemn a man, and quite another to confront his ideas, and there was a general unwillingness (or perhaps inability) to deal with his hypotheses seriously. Predictably, intellectuals from the Center and the Right rallied to De Felice's defense, accusing his critics of ideological lynching. Debate over the book showed signs of becoming a reflection of political divisions in Italy. Help came from a most unexpected source. In a front-page article in a Sunday edition of *l'Unità* (the official communist newspaper), Giorgio Amendola, perhaps the most widely respected communist intel-

lectual, rejected such attacks as Tranfaglia's and
Ferrara's and called for a serious discussion of fascism and antifascism.[8] While he began his article by
announcing his disagreement with De Felice, in the
body of his text Amendola embraced virtually all of
De Felice's major themes, which suggested that he
may have had more than one motive for writing the
article. It seems as if he was saying "this book is no
good" to those who had not followed the debate, yet
delivering a stern lesson to those who had.

Such is the cultural power of the Italian communist
press that Amendola's article almost immediately
calmed the waters, forced many critics to reconsider
their positions, and a rather more serious discussion
ensued. On a television program dealing with the
book, Paolo Spriano, author of the "official" history of
the Italian Communist party, praised De Felice, as
did most of the other historians who appeared on the
program.

There are several important lessons to be drawn
from this debate, but one looms above all: De Felice is
unfortunately right when he speaks of the legacy of a
fascist mentality. The generation that destroyed fascism in Italy was itself indelibly stained by the
enemy, and has carried the stains with it. It is
perhaps too early to expect Italians to undertake a
systematic examination of their recent past (oddly
enough, the Germans, conquered from without, have
been able to accomplish this task faster). Fascist resi-
dues are strong, precisely among those people who
consider themselves to be the most fervent in their
antifascism.

In his short story about Italian fascism, *Mario and
the Magician*, Thomas Mann suggested that in the act
of willing not to do something, there was not enough
room for the idea of freedom. Freedom requires more

20

space, along with a certain tolerance, a willingness to give and take and compromise, which comes with a civil society. One does not automatically become a democrat by joining the ranks of antifascism.

NOTES

1. A. J. P. Taylor, *The Origins of the Second World War* (New York), 1964, p. 59.

2. Cf., for example, P. Cannistraro, *La Fabbrica Del Consenso* (Bari), 1975; J. Thayer, *Italy and the Great War* (Madison), 1964; E. Weber, *Varieties of Fascism* (New York), 1964.

3. Alan Cassels, *Fascism* (New York), 1975, p. 19.

4. Nicola Tranfaglia, "La pugnalata dello storico," in *Il Giorno* (Milan), 6 July 1975. Tranfaglia is professor of history at the University of Turin.

5. Ibid.

6. Giovanni Ferrara, "La pugnalata dello storico," in *Il Giorno*, 9 July 1975. Ferrara is a noted translator of English-language historical and philosophical works.

7. Ibid.

8. Giorgio Amendola, "Per una nuova storia dell'antifascismo," in *l'Unita*, 20 July 1975. Amendola is a member of the Secretariat of the Italian Communist Party.

1
Historical and Theoretical Background of De Felice's Work

Ledeen: Where and with whom did you study Italian history? Who have been the major influences in your development?

De Felice: It is difficult to say who the major influences upon me have been. It is much easier to say with whom I have studied. I studied with and earned my degree with Chabod. I continued to study with him in Naples and then in Rome in the last days of his life. Having said this, however, I must add that I do not believe there are such persons who can be considered the professors or masters of their students: If someone is a student in the strict sense of the word, he is a person with no intellectual autonomy. It is possible to speak of a series of influences. Chabod's influence has been very important in shaping the way I study history, both from the standpoint of methodology and the way in which he posed empirical problems. I knew the Chabod of the lectures, of the seminars in Rome, of the courses in Naples, who worked on the [French] Revolution or on the Renaissance. The "contemporary" Chabod—the Chabod of

Italian foreign policy or of fascism itself—I only knew
through his books, or at best through the stories, the
rumors, or the episodes one heard from his assistants
early in the morning in Naples. Chabod represents
something quite precise and concrete in my development.

There are also other scholars who have been of
primary importance. Their relative importance is
quite different, both from each other and from
Chabod. These are Cantimori—and in a certain sense
I consider myself to be more a student of Cantimori
than of Chabod—and Giuseppe De Luca. My concern
with De Luca is quite simple: De Luca has influenced
me with a kind of historical sensitivity, his history of
the *Pietà,* his method of integration of all kinds of
stimuli and suggestions from literature and the arts,
and his method of the utilization of a series of other
disciplines into historical analysis.

The relationship with Cantimori is perhaps the
most important, especially since I was a young man
when I knew him. I got to know him while I was
working on my thesis, and I continued to have
friendly relations with him, relations that grew ever
closer, notwithstanding the difference between our
ages, up until the time of his death. It is complicated
to define my relationship with Cantimori. At the
beginning of the fifties it was inevitable for a young
man who went to the university to have a certain
fascination for the man who was considered the great
master and patriarch of Marxist historiography in
Italian universities. This aspect was always secon-
dary in my relations with Cantimori. It was based on
a communality of interests.

One of the main historiographical interests of Cantimori concerned a certain aspect of the Enlightenment, the Italian Jacobinism, and I began my histori-

cal research by studying the Italian Jacobins.[1] As this predilection for the Jacobins continued and as I worked in close contact with Cantimori (the second volume on the Italian Jacobins in the series Scrittori d'Italia, published by Laterza,[2] was done in coauthorship) it became increasingly evident—from friendly conversations between the two of us and from various reminiscences of Cantimori and bits of research we did together—that we also shared another interest, an interest in contemporary Italy, an interest in fascism that finally became more precise when I began my work on the Jews. What was most helpful to me in my relationship with Cantimori was the confirmation of certain ideas I had on how to analyze these problems.

Cantimori used to get very angry, especially in private—above and beyond my own memories there are several of his letters in this regard that are very important—with what he called the *sublime moralism* of certain Italian intellectuals. He considered such moralism both irrelevant and dangerous for the study of contemporary history. At the same time he rejected all the pseudopolitical generalizations in the field of contemporary history. Looking at his last writings, even the most episodical ones like those gathered in *Conversando di storia*,[3] we find various hints, various emphases, frequently consisting of two- and three-word phrases, which are typical of the way in which he conceived of contemporary history. For example, with regard to university instruction, he says that this must not consist of liberal democratic sermons, or those of any other ideology or political position. In particular I wish to recall that beautiful letter in which he faced the problem of fascism and said that he was against any and all generalizations: fascism and antifascism are themes without meaning at a historiographical level. Neither constitutes a unity. One must look within and behind these realities. In this connection, I often think of that stupendous page on fascism where Cantimori compares it with the great white whale of *Moby Dick*, saying that it must be considered in all its components and in all its developments.[4]

Ledeen: This brings us to your interest in fascism. How is it that beginning with the Jacobins you arrived at the fascists?

De Felice: This is a complicated subject. I could answer you with a paradox that is profoundly false; nonetheless, like all those things that are profoundly false, it has at its base an element of truth. I have always had—and Cantimori wrote this, too, with regard to an article of mine on Preziosi[5]—a certain taste, a psychological and human interest in a particular kind of personality that is both coherently cold-blooded and Luciferian. There is something in common between my Jacobins and a certain kind of fascism—in particular the fascists of the first years. This element in common is surely false historiographically, but perhaps true psychologically.

There is something even more important than this: I began to get interested in fascism through the study of the Jews under fascism. This, too, is a complicated problem. When I began to study history, one of the great themes—and instead of "great themes" it might be more accurate to say "great fashions"—was the period of the French Revolution, the period of Italian Jacobinism, which was studied in an effort to understand the successive evolution of Italian history, the period of the Risorgimento. That kind of analysis—which interested me then and which continues to interest me even now—could not in the end explain recent developments of Italian history. It was necessary to confront the period of fascism itself and grab it by the throat.

Existing material on the fascist period did not satisfy me because in my work with Chabod and Cantimori I was used to reasoning on the basis of research and documents. It was not possible to write the history of fascism until one had looked at documents of the period. Although I did not entirely reject it, the kind of historiography of fascism written several decades ago was unsatisfactory. Twenty or thirty years ago, fascism was too recent an experience, it was still too hot a subject, and an objective, scientific kind of historical analysis was impossible. Still, I was convinced that the moment had come to attempt a more fully historical analysis, a less political discussion, which could not have been requested of the generation that lived through fascism, fought it, or witnessed it. This would have required a truly exceptional person, a kind of person that I do not believe exists.

Croce's remark to his students at the Institute in Naples is highly symptomatic: "I will not do the history of fascism because it disgusts me; however, if I had to do it, I would do it opposite the current manner."[6] I was convinced that history had to be done in a different way, and that this was the task of the new generation; of those who either had not lived through fascism or had lived it as spectators. They were sufficiently young that they could not have been totally conditioned by the passions of the time. It was necessary to revisit fascism, to restudy it, with greater objectivity and with the greatest critical serenity possible. Fascism, which I call "historical fascism"—that which existed between 1919 and

1945—is dead, and it cannot be revived. It is a closed
chapter, and because of this it is possible to study it
historically, with a historical method and a historical
mentality.[7]

You may say this is a problem that concerns historians. But there was and is a greater problem: an
ethical-political problem. Fascism did great damage,
but one of its most terrible achievements was to leave
an inheritance of a fascist mentality to nonfascists, to
the generation that followed fascism, to those people
who, both in word and in action, are truly and deci-
sively antifascist. This fascist mentality must be
fought in every manner because it is terribly dangerous. It is a mentality of intolerance and of ideological
oppression, which seeks to disqualify its opponents in
order to destroy them.

Ledeen: How did you begin your studies of fascism?
What path has your study of fascism taken?

De Felice: In the context of my eighteenth-century
studies, I became involved in the study of the Jews
during the Napoleonic period.[8] These studies provoked a reaction in the Italian Jewish world, which
then made me an exceptional offer. The leaders of the
Union of Italian Jewish Communities said to me that
since I had done all this work on the Jews of the
eighteenth-century during the Napoleonic period,
and written two articles on anti-Semitism during the
post-World War I period, why did I not do a study of
the Jews during fascism? I replied that this interested me very much, but that there was a big
obstacle—documentation. The information we had
was not sufficient; the testimony of the participants,
while very important, was not enough, and further-
more might lead one into error. There were thorough

collections of journals and newspapers of the period, but this, too, was insufficient. Something else was necessary. Those who were trying to interest me in the project said at this point that they were willing to open up all the archives of the Union of the Italian-Jewish Communities. This was a giant step forward, but it was still not enough. It was necessary to see the official documentation of the Italian state, the government archives, the Fascist archives. Up until that moment no one had managed to gain permission to see these archives.

As a result of a series of circumstances (probably due to the uniqueness of the theme and to its moral importance above and beyond its historical importance), at the end of the fifties I was able to look at all the documentation that concerned the entire Fascist period, including the Social Republic and the Foreign Ministry. I then undertook to write the book, and from this book[9] all the rest was born, in particular the biography of Mussolini. Once I had started work on the problem, it seemed even more necessary to carry the analysis of fascism forward, both for its historical importance and for its cultural, moral, ethical, and indirect political implications. The decision to do a biography of Mussolini was a difficult one even then, because it was clear that this would be an extremely arduous enterprise, if for no other reason than that modern historiography—and in particular modern Italian historiography—did not have much sympathy for biography.

Aside from the fact that I believed in this project and wanted to do it, Cantimori gave me great moral and practical encouragement. He always told me that I had to deal with the project in a manner that I considered proper, and said this to me even when he strongly disagreed with the way I was doing it. He

would say: "I do not agree with you on this and that
point. However, if I have not convinced you, by all
means continue to work in a manner that you consider proper, because it is quite likely that I have
made a mistake. I told you that I do not agree, but you
must not change your work if you are not convinced."
In this way my work went forward, and I am pleased
with the way it is continuing because I believe I am
doing something significant.

If when I began work on Mussolini's biography I
had known exactly what this work was to mean in my
life, I am not sure that I would have done it. At the
beginning of the project I thought I would write four
volumes and that it would take about five or six years
of work. Now I am at the end of the fourth volume
(and some of these, like the last one, go on for a
thousand pages) and there are still two tomes to be
done. Italians had to endure Mussolini and fascism
for twenty years; I have had to endure them for an
additional twenty. Maybe twenty years, maybe even
more—it is a lifetime. I do not know if, once the
biography of Mussolini is done, I shall be able to
finish with fascism and return to my Jacobins and my
men of the Enlightenment. For better or worse, if I
am tied to something, I am tied to these studies on
fascism.

Many people have asked me if I do not get
nauseated by the whole business after a while, if
Mussolini and fascism do not start to come out of my
ears. The answer is no, because in even the tiniest
episodes and most marginal activities, I think I have
found the explanation of very many things, not only
of historical events, but also of things that are happening today. This fascinates me and terrifies me at
the same time. When I say that I think I have found
the explanation of things happening today, I do not

intend to speak about the resurrection of Mussolini or a Mussolini number two, or a new political fascism, rather I am speaking about a psychological fascism. But we shall return to this theme later on.

Ledeen: In the course of your research on fascism, aside from the official Italian archives, the archives of the Fascist state, the archives of the Jewish community, and so on, have you found it useful to speak to some of the personalities, some of the figures who were alive during the fascist period? Are there human archives, men and women who were involved in the fascist period who have been particularly useful to you or particularly important to your research on the fascist period?

De Felice: Aside from really tiny episodes to which three or four lines or a small footnote are dedicated in my biography of Mussolini, oral testimony has not given me anything fundamental in terms of data or evidence for the major explanations I have given of fascism. Memory is a very tricky business, and people's memories deceive them. Recollections are imprecise, and with the passage of time memories of things change, they serve to justify a person's activities and given the perspective of thirty, forty, or fifty years, they undergo substantial modification. Oral testimony has given me a great deal of assistance in understanding the atmosphere, people's behavior, various states of mind, and attitudes. It also provided an ideal of the major personalities. This sort of thing has been enormously important for me. It has given me both the opportunity to become sensitized to certain problems, and the motivation to search for additional documentation in many areas. From this point of view people like Nenni or Grandi, like De

Stefani or Ottavio Pastore, like Cesare Rossi or
Alfonso Leonetti have been extremely useful. To explain this better I would like to take three cases, each
very different and yet extremely typical. Anybody
who has read my biography of Mussolini must have
realized that, much as I tried to be critical and objective, there are certain positions and persons whom I
cannot humanly treat dispassionately. There is a
psychological and moral incomprehension on my
part. The Nationalists are a major element in this
category. Often they seem ingenuous, naive, and
stupid, even if I have to recognize the great intellectual acumen of Rocco. This difficulty of understanding them humanly was confirmed in an event that
took place a few years ago. In the course of my work I
have gone to all the people that I could possibly find in
my search for documentation of the fascist period.
Most of them showed me the documentation that they
had; some tried to fool me, some spoke at great length,
some showed me very little or virtually nothing.
However, this almost invariably took place on a very
civilized plane. Only one person refused not only to
show me the documentation he had, but also refused
even to see me, saying that he could not do so for a
variety of reasons. Ostensibly these were the reasons,
the true reason being that we were—as he later wrote
to me—on two different sides of the barricade. I was
dealing with a combative mentality, with someone
who absolutely refused to embark upon a historical
analysis. It is typical that he was a nationalist. It was
Federzoni. It is possible that the negative picture I
have drawn of Italian nationalism corresponds in
part to the incapacity I have discovered in those
members of its major exponents that I have known
that even attempt to come to the level of historical
analysis after all these years. This represents a lack

of coherence and dignity in the face of their defeat. It is a posthumous demonstration that Italian nationalism was more a moral and psychological attitude than a political position, an attitude that completely lacked the capacity of measuring itself effectively against the Italian society of its time and then taking a realistic position in the face of that reality.

There is another case completely different from that of Federzoni, which refers not to the biography of Mussolini but to the book on the Jews. I had the great fortune to speak at length—an entire afternoon one winter—with Margherita Grassini Sarfatti shortly before she died. From this conversation I learned absolutely nothing in terms of factual or documentary discovery. However, it was an enormous benefit to see this woman and to understand the kind of influence that she must have had for several years. After that conversation, I asked myself how much of the myth of "Rome and Romanness" came from Mussolini, and how much was due to Grassini Sarfatti's influence. I had never met anyone so obsessed with Romanness.

Years ago someone suggested that after I finished my biography of Mussolini I should write a book about the "personalities of an epoch." Since I had met so many of the personages of fascism and antifascism who have died off one by one in the course of time, it was suggested that I write a book containing thumbnail sketches of those personalities. But to do a book of this sort one needs someone who writes well in this genre, and I do not. Even if I were capable I would not do it, because there are certain rules of civilized life that must be respected. These people have been correct and courteous with me and I see no reason why I should repay them by writing portraits of them that would inevitably emphasize those aspects of

their personalities that most impressed me. Therefore, I am not going to tell you any of the episodes that
took place during my meeting with Grassini Sarfatti.
What is important is that these episodes were extremely indicative and useful to my understanding
Grassini Sarfatti, the kind of mentality and importance she must have had for Mussolini.

Let me provide you with one more example. I knew
a person who, through his family, was in very close
contact with Preziosi. After the death of his father,
who had been one of Preziosi's teachers, the two
families had remained very friendly. At the beginning of the racial campaign against the Jews, there
were various discussions among these friends and
Preziosi (here I must mention that Preziosi had
adopted an orphan). In the course of one of these
discussions, the person of whom I am speaking said to
Preziosi: "But has it never occurred to you that your
son might be a Jew?" This person said to me that
Preziosi acted as if he had been struck by lightning,
that this thought had never occurred to him, that he
had never considered this possibility. The friendship
between the two men ended at that very moment.
This story helps explain Preziosi to me. To return to
your question: It is only from this point of view that
interviews have been useful to me. From the point of
view of documentation, they are at least ninety-five
percent useless.

Ledeen: In the course of all the interviews you have
conducted, was there any key personality? Has there
been any one person who has unlocked a whole series
of doors to you in your research?

De Felice: If I had to make a list of all the people I
have interviewed in the course of my work, it would

never end. For example, I interviewed Giuriati, the secretary of the Fascist party, who had previously been chief of D'Annunzio's cabinet in Fiume. He was ninety years old. We spoke, and he showed me the unpublished part of his memoirs and the documents he had. I also had very interesting conversations with Nenni, dealing with the relations between him and Mussolini when they were young. The same holds true for Grandi, De Stefani, and Cini. But one of the people whom I knew best, in the sense that I continued to talk with him after having "exploited" him, long after I had seen the few documents that he had, and long after he had finished telling me everything he remembered, was Cesare Rossi.

It was an extremely interesting experience, because the reactions of this man (who, when I knew him, was old and sick) are indicative of the tremendous shock and sense of rupture that the Matteotti case had. With Cesare Rossi it was possible to talk about anything and everything with extreme detachment. In particular, we discussed the period up until 1924 and, for the little information he had, the period afterward. But when the discussion came to the Matteotti case, Rossi's reaction was either rage or tears. He lost his calm and began to cry, flew into a rage, and pounded his fists on the table. The human problem with this man continues to impress me even today, because he was sincere. He suffered from the doubts others had regarding his own guilt, doubts that remained even in those who had, like me, studied the problem and understood that Rossi had nothing directly to do with it.

This suffering of Rossi's, this torment of his came out in the most unbelievable ways. I would like to give you an example. Cesare Rossi had given me all kinds of presents, but most important, those few

books which he had had in prison. I was very insistent
that he give me something for my gallery of
horrors—something with no historical value
whatsoever—a photograph made to serve as a postcard that had been mailed to him, showing two or
three kittens in a baby crib. This postcard had a
greeting on the other side from a friend who was not
exactly a friend; I do not know exactly how to describe
the relationship between the two men because I never
saw them together. This person was very excited because his cat had kittens; he was so excited that he
photographed them in a baby crib and sent the photograph to Rossi. It was a poetic relationship. The man
was Amerigo Dumini.

It is an entire world. I do not know what sort of man
Dumini was because I never knew him. But insofar as
Rossi was concerned, many of his troubles came directly from Dumini; and yet after getting out of
prison he reestablished relations with this man, and
Dumini felt the necessity of sending Rossi the postcard. Now you can understand why I wanted this
postcard for my gallery of horrors. These strange
people have always interested me; humanity is also
made up of strange people.

Ledeen: In this connection Mosse once said to me
that perhaps the person who was most important to
him for his research on nazism was Speer, not because Speer told him things that were new and significant, but because Speer managed to explain to Mosse
the fascination that Hitler had as a man, as a personality. Speer enabled Mosse to understand the atmosphere around the Führer. He clarified exactly how it
was that Hitler moved inside these groups, how the
myth of the Führer was created, the myth of the man
who never made a mistake, who knew everything,

who hypnotized everyone. This is more or less the same thing that you have discovered through the personalities that you have interviewed, is it not?

De Felice: This discussion about the interviews could go on indefinitely. I would like to cite just one other case that can serve as an example of all the rest. Permit me not to name names; it is better not to do it, in this world of wolves that is Italian political life.

The case of Cesare Rossi is illustrative. It is an example of a fascist, even with all the changes and dreadful experiences he went through under fascism: prison, exile, and so forth. Instead, I would like to talk about my experiences with one of the leaders of antifascism—not, however, one of the leaders of the second generation who fought fascism purely as one fights an enemy. This man was one of those who had fought Mussolini after having been a friend of his during his youth. Even in the total rejection and condemnation of Mussolini, I still heard the echo of a friendship that had obviously been canceled by the political events of the preceding thirty or forty years, but after all was said and done, still remained. It was as if this man wanted to say: "He was our leader. He was the one who represented us best. All of us recognized ourselves in him." This person even today is tortured in the most intimate part of his being by the question of whether during certain situations of his life as an antifascist, Mussolini helped him. He wants to know. One of the things he most wants to know before he dies is whether he owes Mussolini something: neither because he feels guilty nor indebted, but because he wonders whether that old friendship, notwithstanding all the struggles and the opposition and the hate, at the very bottom of everything, had survived.

2
Seeking a Definition of Fascism

Ledeen: A few years ago, in your book *The Interpretations of Fascism*, you wrote that at that time one could undertake a provisional first approximation on the subject of fascism. Now, after having written *Mussolini the Duce: The Years of the Consensus*, do you think it is impossible to undertake something more definitive or are we still at the previous state of affairs?

De Felice: I do not want to appear to be either hypocritical or masochistic, but I would say no. I do not believe the work I have done is of sufficient value to resolve the problem. Historiography on fascism or on the various fascisms (even though the material on nazism and Germany is much further advanced than it is on Italian fascism), for the volume of works and for the level of understanding achieved, is still in a preliminary phase.[10] We are still so many Madame de Staëls.

Ledeen: What do you mean by that?

De Felice: In the history of the French Revolution, Madame de Staël represents the beginning of historiography. We, too, have barely come out of the polemical period and are now beginning to take our first steps in the field of historiography. We are still at the Madame de Staël stage, therefore before Michelet, before Thiers. As we say in Italian: The horse waits until the grass grows! And we cannot even begin to talk of arriving at the level of Mathiez or of Lefebvre or of Furet, because we are so remote from them that it is better not even to attempt a comparison.

As Tasca has written: To interpret fascism is to write its history. So let us first do the history of fascism, and then later on we shall try to interpret it. Every one of us who works in this field moves in a particular interpretive tradition: It is true of me and, above all, of my opposition. The difference between us resides in the fact that my opposition is convinced that its interpretive method is the right one; its exponents distribute it in the piazzas and they want everyone to accept it as indubitable. I have limited myself to presenting my interpretation to my readers as an ongoing conquest. I have my editorial agreements with Einaudi, and at the end of this monstrous biography of Mussolini in six volumes—Mussolini in five thousand pages—I have promised to write an abridged Mussolini, a Mussolini...

Ledeen: In three hundred pages?

De Felice: No. Not three hundred, but perhaps five, six, or eight hundred pages at most. I am convinced this Mussolini will be a different Mussolini, and I do not feel any guilt about it. Historians who make a

statement when they are twenty, twenty-five, or
thirty years old and then repeat the same thing when
they are seventy are almost invariably mediocrities.
It is very rare that a claim that is not purely factual
should remain valid over a long period of time, either
because our objective knowledge grows or becomes
more precise, because one grows more mature as one
grows older, or because the entire context of historical studies makes progress. Earlier I spoke about the
opposition. I would be the last to say that everything
they say is erroneous. I am not in agreement with the
central theme of their historical argument, but many
of the specific things they have said are very important and must be taken into consideration.

My abridged Mussolini as compared to the full-
length Mussolini might very well be quite different in
many ways. After all, it will have been written
twenty years after I began work on the subject. One
has to be sufficiently modest to recognize this evolution. What I write is true only at the level of understanding I had at the time of writing. There has been
a long series of judgments pronounced on my work
during the course of the past ten or fifteen years. The
second volume, but also the third, the second part of
Mussolini the Fascist, was defined as *most mature*
when it came out. The first volume of *The Duce*,
which has come out now, has also been defined as
most mature. I very much hope that the same thing
will be said of the last volume, *The Ally*. I would like
to do new editions of all these books—I have already
asked my editor, Einaudi. The revisions that I might
undertake can only be factual. Every now and then
they will have something to do with interpretive
problems, but changes in the interpretive structure
can only be limited. At the very end of all this work, I
shall be able to rethink the entire problem from be-

ginning to end, and this might very well bring me to reconsider many of my judgments.

The historian cannot remain attached like an oyster to its shell. If he does he is no longer a historian; he is either a politician or a theologian. One must write history day by day with continuous acquisitions. Every book at the very moment it is published, in a certain sense, is rejected by the author, because as he rethinks it he will have something more, something different to say. It is this that brings life to our work. Contemporary Italian history is sick from oversecurity.

Ledeen: Could you expand on that a little?

De Felice: Contemporary Italian history is too confident, too dogmatic. From the methodological point of view as well—this is a word I hate, because it is too pompous and is used too often—what I am saying might prove to be useful, especially for younger scholars interested in this field. We know virtually nothing for sure, nothing is certain. Every day, day by day, we seek to conquer some bit of truth; every day we try to approximate a little bit more of the truth, to draw closer to it.

Ledeen: Could you attempt at least a temporary approximation of fascism? You have said it is not possible in your view to draw a definitive picture of it. However, certain fundamental points, certain themes have been identified by you and by others.

De Felice: They have been identified up to a certain point. Let me give you an example. I am a great admirer of Mosse's most recent book,[11] on nationalization of the masses, which is of great importance. I

wrote the introduction for the Italian edition of this
work, in which I said—with all the provisos that one
can make in these cases—that there are only two
works with which it can be compared, culturally
speaking (I am not referring here about the method
but rather the effects that these works have): Huizinga's *Waning of the Middle Ages*[12] and *Les Rois
Thaumaturgues* by Marc Bloch.[13]

At the present state of our knowledge of fascism
and of Italy from unification to the present—that is to
say a tiny fraction compared to what Mosse had to
know to prove his point—Mosse's analyses are not
applicable to Italy. They would not be applicable to
Italy even if one studied all those particular aspects
that Mosse studied in the case of Germany: one would
reach the conclusion that in Italy these things did not
exist, or if they did they were so weak as to have been
insignificant.

The discussion of the *New Politics*[14] is a German
discussion. It would be useful to discuss the possibility of applying this analysis to other countries; it
certainly cannot be applied to Italy. The analysis
reveals itself in its full significance and value in the
case of Germany, and as it is applied to other countries it loses in importance. For Italy, this phenomenon is not applicable; this kind of "nationalization of
the masses,"[15] to use Mosse's words, this "new politics" did not exist in Italy; therefore the entire discussion changes. This is decisive. This does not change
the fact that Mosse's book is basic for understanding
Italian fascism, not just nazism, because it provides a
dramatic contrast. It confirms one of my fundamental
ideas that there are enormous differences between
Italian fascism and German national socialism. They
are two worlds, two traditions, two histories. They
are so different that it is extremely difficult to reunite

them in a single discussion. It is not impossible to find a common denominator; however, we must identify it and establish it clearly and concretely. I can offer some hypotheses, suggest a minimum common denominator. It would require many more studies, many more very serious, profound, and concrete analyses to establish this minimum common denominator. This is why I am opposed to generalizations. In the present phase—excuse me now if I exhort my countrymen in a manner that will appear masochistic and reductive and that will arouse great polemics, sarcastic remarks, and great rages—we must be erudite. Let us make of ourselves scholars of our national history; let us publish the documents and clarify the facts. Part of a very widespread historiography about fascism has undertaken an operation that, to use a metaphor, I would define as the *construction of skyscrapers out of pile embankments*. If we look at the audience that certain books have, we see that the skyscrapers built on pile embankments have an audience that lives in little caves and passes from the caves to the pile embankment and deludes itself into thinking that it has moved into the glorious skyscrapers of New York or Havana. Instead, alas, they are only little cave dwellers who have barely made it into the pile embankments.

Ledeen: I had hoped you would say that today something more than a first approximation could be undertaken, at least insofar as Italian fascism is concerned. Having written *Mussolini the Duce*, did you not believe you were saying something more durable, more fundamental? At least in its basic outlines, have we not learned something about Italian fascism? Can we not begin to say something aside from the specific details of the history of fascism?

De Felice: I have made an effort to write a kind of synthesis from this point of view, but it has not been published yet. I have written a section on fascism for a new major undertaking of the *Italian Encyclopedia*, the *Encyclopedia* of the nineteen-hundreds. The section is an attempt—presumptuous and modest at the same time—to put together my thoughts on fascism. One can undertake this discussion, but I do not know to what extent it is proper.

What is the point of this conversation of ours? What is it good for? Does it serve to fossilize, to freeze, to photograph Renzo De Felice and what he thinks about fascism in February 1975? Or does it contribute to the discussion of these themes? I wish to high heaven that it were this; until now, the only timid attempt at discussion was undertaken in 1967 in the *Rivista Storica Italiana*, between Vivarelli and Valiani.[16] From that moment on, any real analysis has ended. There have been reviews in scientific journals, newspapers, magazines, and other publications. There have been endless reviews of this sort. But no one in Italy has undertaken a serious discussion either of my *Mussolini* or of my *Interpretations of Fascism*. From a certain point of view I find this very satisfying, because it means that (notwithstanding all the insults, challenges, the yelling; notwithstanding all the accusations even of fascism that have been aimed at me by people who do not understand either the way things are or that a criticism of Mussolini today must be directed not polemically but historically) no one has wanted to undertake a serious discussion at a scientific or at a political level. That is to say at a really profound political level, not on that oversimplified level of fascism or antifascism that is unacceptable for an analysis of this type, but serves only for those speeches and comments that one makes in piazzas and at mass ralleys.

3
General Characteristics of Fascism

Ledeen: The moment has come to undertake a discussion of the major themes of fascism—first of Italian fascism, then of fascism in general. In the literature on fascism, many historians have made a distinction between fascism as movement and fascism as regime. What is your opinion?

De Felice: This is an important theme that must be developed both to undertake a comparative analysis of the various fascisms and as an extreme case to discuss neofascism. Indeed, it is the fundamental problem. But there is a long series of distinctions that must be made. To start with, you say this is a problem that has been raised by many people. Where? Outside Italy! Italian historiography has not faced the problem of fascism as movement and fascism as regime. It is a theme that Italian historical culture and Italian political culture have never faced, or at most, they have only touched on it. Do you not agree?

Ledeen: Yes. However, the fact remains that in the literature and in the historiography on fascism in

France, England, Germany, and the United States, it
is one of the fundamental themes.

De Felice: It is necessary to make a distinction between Italian historical culture, Italian culture as
such, and that of the other countries. It is important
because there is a different conditioning with regard
to these problems in Italy compared to that which
exists abroad. This theme is fundamental, because
fascism as movement is a constant in the history of
fascism; a constant that loses importance as time
progresses, it loses hegemony and becomes secon-
dary; but it is always present. Fascism as movement
is the "red thread" that connects March 1919 with
April 1945; fascism as regime, fascism as party, is
something quite different. As far as fascism as
movement is concerned, there are certain phases,
periods, elements, but they are a continuum, notwithstanding their diversity. Within fascism as regime there are fractures of a more fundamental sort.
Fascism as movement is that part of fascism that has
a certain vitality. With this I do not want to present a
positive evaluation of it, an evaluation of merit; I
simply want to make a statement of fact about the
vitality of fascism, while the party, the regime, represents its negation in certain respects.

Ledeen: Could you please expand on this?

De Felice: Fascism as movement is the impulse to
renew, to interpret certain needs, certain stimuli,
and certain themes of renovation. It is that spark of
revolutionary fervor that there is within fascism itself, and that tends to construct something new. It is a
collection of elements, above all cultural (conscious
and unconscious) and psychological, which in part
belong to the intransigent fascism that predates the

march on Rome, but in part represent something new and different, which developed only afterward. These elements constitute the self-representation of fascism projected into the future, above and beyond the actual conditions it brought about, the fears, the defeats imposed by the regime, above and beyond even the life of Mussolini himself. In this context it is the fundamental component for the understanding of the consensus; it is the moral component, alongside the material one (that of security, which I analyzed in my last volume). Fascism as regime, on the other hand, is the politics of Mussolini, it is the result of a political program that—whether desired or not—tended to make fascism just the superstructure of the personal power of a dictatorship, of a political line that in many ways became merely the inheritance of a tradition.

This discussion of continuity and fracture, which today is used so often for the history of Italy with regard to prefascism, fascism, and postfascism, is elaborated through the discussion of fascism as regime. Fascism as movement jumps the entire problem. It has a line that constitutes a clean break between fascism and postfascism. Fascism as movement is fracture. The regime is continuity. Postfascism is a continuity of the regime and not of the movement. This may be a play on words, but I do not believe so.

Ledeen: No, I agree that this is a very important distinction. But could you please be a bit more precise about exactly what you have in mind when you speak of fascism as movement?

De Felice: Fascism as movement was the idealization, the desire of an emerging middle class. Here lies the point on which I differ from many other scholars of these problems: An emerging middle class that tends to activate its own political desires in first person. I say "emerging" because in general this discussion—which has been pursued at great length (I think of *Nazionalfascismo* by Salvatorelli,[17] or of Cappa,[18] or of all the literature that has developed around this thesis from the first years of fascism and afterward)—has been based upon one fundamental presupposition: That middle classes were becoming déclassé, proletarianized, and to avoid this fate, they rebelled. Fascism was conceived of as a movement of those people who were being pushed down, a movement of failures. I do not question that there were many people of this sort involved in fascism, but they were the fringes. Fascism as movement was in large part the expression of an emerging middle class, of bourgeois elements who, having become an important social force, attempted to participate and to acquire political power. As its ranks swelled, fascism opened up to all social classes, but its backbone—both quantitatively and insofar as its leadership and the elements that were most active politically and militarily are concerned—is characterized as a petite bourgeois phenomenon, giving to the whole movement (and to the party that followed, at least up until the purges conducted by Augusto Turati in the second half of the twenties) the character of a phenomenon with class aspects.

This explains the insignificant penetration that fascism had in the more traditional regions of Italy, where the petite bourgeoisie was not a modern one, and was therefore more integrated. This class character gave to fascism as movement the possibility of providing the most important point of reference and attraction for those sectors of the petite bourgeois that desired a greater participation in and direction of the political and social life of the country. These sectors no longer recognized the traditional ruling class (and in particular the political class of the country) as capable of governing legitimately and thus, albeit in a confused manner, they challenged the social forces that the ruling classes represented. World War I mobilized an entire sector of Italian society that up until that movement had remained excluded. This sector, mobilized for the war (though excluded from effective power and from political participation), later attempted to acquire and achieve a function of its own through fascism.

Ledeen: What kind of world did these middle classes mobilized by the war want to create?

De Felice: Salvatorelli is right when he talks about middle classes trapped between proletariat and the grande bourgeoisis; but Guido Dorso[19] is even closer to the truth in his book when he beautifully describes the dynamism of these classes in those years: The dynamism, but also the errors, frustrations, and crises. It is not an accident that Dorso, who, immediately following the Liberation, had great success in Italian culture—look at the publication of his works by Einaudi—today has almost completely disappeared from cultural discussions in Italy, because his analysis does not fit with a certain kind of vision of the Italian crisis of that period.

Ledeen: Excuse me if I go back to my original question. Is it possible to briefly summarize exactly what these elements of the middle classes wanted after the war? Is it possible to describe the world that they wanted to create?

De Felice: In terms most readily understood by contemporary culture, these elements asserted them-

selves as a class seeking to gain power and to assert
its own function, its own culture, and its own political
power against both the bourgeoisie and the proletariat. To put the matter briefly: They wanted a
revolution. The revolution of the middle classes is
extremely important. Today, for example, in the Italy
of 1974-75, the central problem of the parties—of the
Christian Democrats, the Socialists, the Communists—is the middle classes. Not only do they exist,
but they are also not marginal, senile, or losing importance, as was said for quite a long time. They are
one of the most important forces of a modern pluralis-
tic, industrialized society.[20] This is the problem, not
just today, but also in the period that followed World
War I, and it is no coincidence that the fascists posed
this problem. The only attempt to create a new antifascist party, a truly new party, not an attempt to
reactivate some already existing movement or
theme—the Unione Nazionale of Amendola[21]—is
born precisely from the analysis of the middle classes.

It was recognized at a certain point that the battle
against fascism would be won or lost on the battle-
ground of the middle classes, and not on other battle-
grounds. This problem is not one that concerns only
1924, 1925, or the Unione Nazionale: It was raised
again following the Liberation by some political
forces, and in particular by the Partito d' Azione, the
Action party. I am not a supporter of the Action party
for a thousand reasons, but one of its great merits was
that it understood that the political analysis of
Italy—and not just of Italy, but of contemporary society in general—hinges on the problem of the middle
classes. It is not a problem that is slowly disappear-
ing, as a certain type of Marxism maintains; quite the
contrary, it is becoming increasingly important

thanks to the embourgeoisement of large sectors of the proletariat.

Fascism was therefore the attempt of the petite bourgeoisie in its ascendancy—not in crisis—to assert itself as a new class, a new force. Fascism as movement was an attempt to put forward new "modern" solutions and "more adequate" methods. This explains a certain kind of corporativism as well, of "interclassism," of a modern type. By "modern," I certainly do not intend to convey a positive evaluation. But you cannot do away with it by saying that it is a medieval kind of corporativism, or a corporativism that comes either from the Renaissance or from Toniolo's corporativism, a Catholic one. Corporativism has a certain ideological and cultural value, which one can either accept or reject—I reject it. But it cannot be simply thrown out and disqualified for the little and the evil it did. One must analyze corporativism itself, and not the fascist corporations as they finally took shape, because if we do this we shift grounds from fascism as movement to fascist as regime.

D'Annunzian corporativism[22] is much more a corporativism as movement than a corporativism as regime; in fact, fascism as regime rejects it and reduces the corporation to a mere administrative instrument that no longer has the importance—even at the level of desires—fascism as movement gave it. But I would like to hear your opinion of these questions.

Ledeen: I would make a somewhat different distinction between fascism as movement and fascism as regime. In my opinion fascism as movement is tied very closely to the war, and must be considered as such from an ideological point of view as well. I completely agree with you that fascism as movement is a movement of emerging levels of the middle class. It does not appear to have been solely a movement of self-defense. It was not—as many have written— merely a movement of defense against the presumed revolutionary menace from the proletariat. Undoubtedly, there was a great deal of fear of the revolution coming from the Left, but there was another perhaps even greater fear in Italy and especially in the Italian government in the years immediately following the war: That of a revolution of those who had fought the war. It was not just a fear of proletarian revolution.

In those years there was a pseudorevolutionary movement in Italy that attempted to impose the values of the war upon the nation. The concept was more or less this: The victory in the war had made it possible to identify the most valid, most virile, and most heroic elements in the population; those who had reacted best to the test of the war were now entitled to take their place in the sun and to assume control of the country. In this connection D'Annunzio's Fiume adventure is typical; I would almost say it is the symbol of the movement. These people—and I agree we are talking about an emerging class—wanted to transform Italy. And I would insist on connecting these with the ideals or the pseudoideals of the war itself.[23]

De Felice: I agree entirely. The fact remains that one can undertake a more general discussion on this basis that might be useful in identifying a minimum common denominator among European fascisms. Even if what I am about to say might appear monstrous to some, is Walter Rathenau so very far removed from this discussion?

Ledeen: No, not so very far removed.

De Felice: At a certain cultural level, when one mentions Rathenau one is talking about a murdered democrat, someone assassinated by the reactionary German Right. But the fact that he was murdered by the Right does nothing to change the fact that his position was similar in many ways to that which we have called *fascism as movement* (it is certainly very far removed from fascism as regime). I do not know if you agree with this.

Ledeen: Yes, I agree fully. At this point, we have reached the moment when we have to talk about the fracture between fascism as regime and fascism as movement. We could undertake this on two levels: On the ideological level, and in part we have already started to do that; and concerning the possibility of talking about a kind of betrayal of fascism as movement by the regime.

De Felice: But all revolutions have been betrayed, at least from someone's point of view. Thermidor, the Directory betrayed the revolution. Trotsky wrote *The Revolution Betrayed*.[24]

Ledeen: Just as the American Constitution betrayed the American Revolution.

De Felice: Exactly, you confirm what I am saying. The fascists of Salò said that fascism as regime had betrayed the ideals of fascism as movement. It is all a question of the relationship between reality and the idea of this reality. The movement is the idea of the reality; the party and the regime are the realization of this reality with all of the objective difficulties that this entails. Fascism as movement had to be realized day by day, at a political level, in a society where the emerging profascist strata of the middle class (a part was antifascist) were not alone, in a vacuum.

Here the personality of Mussolini enters into the game, and it is decisive in understanding fascism. Movement, regime are all true and important elements that must be studied and kept in mind as explanations; but Mussolini is the unifying thread, the element of synthesis. Quite aside from the necessity of picking a line of attack and circumscribing the material, this is one of the principle motives that led me to write the biography of Mussolini, and not the history of fascism, or worse, of Italy under fascism.

Ledeen: So do you think it is fair to talk about a betrayal of the fascist movement, as many of the original fascists maintained?

De Felice: I do not believe in all of these revolutions betrayed, ideologies betrayed, resistances betrayed, and not just in the case of fascism. All of these generalizations are historically misguided. I do not believe that it is possible to impose generalizations of this sort for phenomena of such complexity. In those historical circumstances (every phenomenon is the result of innumerable causes and components) certain solutions that later on are proclaimed betrayed, could not be put into action, or, if they could be attempted, they did not find someone who was able to do it (and not by accident). To speak therefore, as many of the original fascists did, of betrayal is historically unacceptable, a purely polemical argument.

When Mussolini came to power in October 1922 it was the result of a compromise between fascism and the traditional ruling class. From this compromise

comes the character of the coalition that characterized the Mussolini government until 1925. This
compromise was renewed and reinforced at the beginning of 1925, when the bulk of the traditional
ruling class decided to support Mussolini in order to
avoid the danger of a "leap into the blue" after the
crisis produced by the murder of Matteotti. For the
traditional ruling class, fascism was not called upon
to perform great innovations within the system: It
had to reinforce it and "redynamize" it. Above all it
was not to subvert it. But this outlook was unacceptable to fascism, at least for a great part of fascism as
movement, which not only desired greater participation, but also conceived of itself as a genuine alterna-
tive to the traditional ruling class (above all to the
traditional-political ruling class). Consequently,
throughout the first phase of the Mussolini government, there was a counterpoint between the intransigents (who wanted the "second wave" that would
have guaranteed the triumph of fascism as movement) and the flankers (who wanted "normaliza-
tion"). This conflict created many difficulties for
Mussolini, but in the end it saved him politically,
since at the time of the Matteotti crisis, the old intransigents constituted the only real force that remained loyal to him. By their very presence, the
intransigents helped to force a great part of the ruling
class to continue on the road of the compromise
realized two years before. Between the "leap into the
blue"—which in one way or another would have inevitably compromised their moral, political, and economic positions—and Mussolini, the flankers—
preoccupied above all with safeguarding their position and therefore the structures of the traditional
system of which they were an expression (and that by
now they were no longer capable of defending by

themselves against the attack that was moved against them from other sectors of Italian society)—chose Mussolini. In so doing they attempted to repeat on another level the operations that had failed them between the period of the march on Rome and the Matteotti murder. At that time they had tried to revitalize themselves with a fascism that they had sought in vain to constitutionalize and to absorb into the system; now they attempted to save at least the essential structures of the system, aiming to wrap Mussolini in it and along with him the largest possible part of fascism as movement in exchange for their renunciation of a purely political administration of power.

Ledeen: Before one can even talk about betrayal, it is necessary to talk about the reality that was purportedly betrayed. In your view, is it correct to speak of fascism as a revolutionary phenomenon?

De Felice: Regardless of what many people say, yes. However, a revolution in the etymological sense of the word, because if one gives the word a moral or positive value, or if one refers to a Leninist conception of the term, then it is clear that fascism was not a revolution. It is a mistake to assign such criteria to all phenomena. Fascism was a revolutionary phenomenon, if for no other reason than because it created a regime, and even more, a movement—and here we have to remember the qualitative difference between the regime and that which the movement wanted it to be—which aimed at the mobilization of the masses and the creation of a new kind of man. When it is said that the fascism regime was conservative, authoritarian, or reactionary, this may be true. However, it had nothing in common with the conservative regimes that existed prior to fascism or with the reactionary regimes that have come after it.

For example, it may be politically useful to define the regime of the Greek colonels as a fascist regime, and the same may be said of the Chilean military government. However, this is useful only as a political slogan. Both the Greek and the Chilean regimes are based on the classic reactionary-authoritarian systems of the nineteenth century and are therefore regimes that tend toward the demobilization of the masses. They seek the passive participation of the masses in the regime. It is not an accident that neither the Greek colonels nor the Chilean military have created a mass party.

The fascist regime has a central element that distinguishes it from reactionary and conservative regimes: The mobilization and active participation of the masses. That this participation later takes a demagogical form is another matter; the principle remains one of active participation, not exclusion. This is one of the revolutionary elements. Another revolutionary element is that Italian fascism wanted to achieve the transformation of society and the individual in a direction that had never been attempted or realized in the past.

Conservative regimes have a model that belongs to the past and that must be recuperated and reinstituted, a model that they maintain is still valid and that was only interrupted by a revolutionary act. They desire, therefore, to return to the prerevolutionary situation. Regimes of the fascist type on the other hand want to create something that constitutes a new phase in the history of civilization.

Here we must introduce a differentiation between fascism in its Italian version and German national socialism. While nazism has a revolutionary appearance through its mobilization of the masses, insofar as the transformation of society is concerned it moves on a double path different from the Italian case. It seems to create a new society, but the most profound values on which this society must be created are traditional, antique, and unchangeable. The principle of race is typical, but it is not the only one. All the research and analysis of Mosse on the "new politics" of nazism demonstrate that nazism did not do anything other than recuperate and adapt the "new politics" exactly as it had developed from the anti-Napoleonic wars onward. Nazism sought a restoration of values and not the creation of new values. The idea of the creation of a new kind of man is not a nazi idea.

Ledeen: It is a matter of liberating the German man...

De Felice: ... from the superstructures he has accumulated in the past. This does not exist in Italian fascism.

Ledeen: For the Germans, the man of the future already existed, indeed he had always existed. He had been suffocated by modernity: The last two centuries weighed heavily on Aryan man. The mission of German national socialism was destroying these modern elements and liberating the Ayran man; while the fascists wanted to do something quite different indeed.

De Felice: I am in perfect agreement with you. Here lies the fundamental difference between nazism and Italian fascism.

Ledeen: Before we go deeper into the subject, I would like to ask you another question about the origins of Italian fascism and of fascism in general. In your book on the *Interpretations of Fascism*, you wrote that the triumph of fascism was not inevitable, that it was certainly not a necessity, and that the ruling classes in both Italy and Germany committed grave errors in dealing with the fascist movement. It would be useful to list these errors and examine the relationship between the political and social forces of prefascist society with the fascist movement.

De Felice: Let me take the case of Germany first. The responsibility of the German ruling class for the success of fascism is far inferior to that of the Italian ruling class. The only point at which I consider the German ruling class to be responsible is that in contrast to the Italian ruling class the Germans knew what fascism was, because Italian fascism had already existed for ten years. However, in Germany the objective situation was such that it was much more difficult to contain the drive of nazism toward power. It is enough to think of the crisis of German society, a political crisis in the historical sense, as a result of the defeat in World War I, of the internal political consequences of the period between the end of the war and Hitler's capture of power, of the economic situation as it developed as a result of the great American crisis, and, finally, of the process of nationalization of the masses, in the sense that Mosse uses the phrase.

Let us return then to the Italian case. When I speak of gross responsibilities on the part of the Italian ruling class, and when I deny the inevitability of the part of the Italian ruling class, and when I deny the seizure of power by fascism, I mean that in 1922, precisely when fascism takes power, all the conditions that favored it and determined its emergence and success were by now in decline. The economic situation was improving; the threat—which had so terrified the Italian bourgeoisie—of seizure of power by the Left had by now vanished; the danger of a rupture of the nationalist bloc was increasingly less real (on the contrary, there were symptoms that could lead one to believe that the nationalist camp could recuperate important fringes of that electorate which in preceding years had been led by the Left and in particular by the Socialist party). There was a very strong possibility that the reformist socialists of Turati and Matteotti could form part of a bourgeois-democratic government.

Here is where the grave responsibilities of the Italian ruling classes lie: In not having had the courage to carry forward a policy that would have been courageous—and that could have been easily realized—and in having fallen back upon a solution that appeared to be easier and more in keeping with Italian tradition. They acted with a complete lack of political imagination and with a complete incapacity of assuming true responsibilities. They adopted a policy of constitutionalizing fascism, of taking a transfusion from fascism, while at the same time attempting to emasculate and deprive it of its subversive and anticonstitutional dynamism. It was the same game that the old liberal state had played in the past, when it constitutionalized the republicans and a part of socialism, reforming it, and when it "Gentilonized"[25] the Catholic opposition.

This policy was one of inserting their opponents one by one in their own ranks, as governing groups. All of these operations were carried out at the level of leadership; it was among the leaders of these parties that the liberal state created space, certainly not at the level of the masses, but at the base. It is here that one finds the true failure of *trasformismo* and of Giolittism in this maneuver, absorbing the leadership without having the capacity to integrate the masses into the state, masses who at one time identified with this leadership. The old game was tried once again with fascism. It is an operation that we are seeing again today when a sector of the Italian bourgeoisie talks about the participation of communists in power, thinking that this means transforming them into social democrats.

The same kind of reasoning was undertaken for the fascists by the men of 1922, with the mitigating circumstance that aside from sporadic and relatively unimportant cases, the ruling class of the time did not have the vaguest idea of what fascism was and how impossible it was to truly constitutionalize it.

To a certain extent fascism *was* constitutionalized; it was rendered impotent and ineffective. For this reason the power structure at the level of the classes that held power was not substantially modified. However, if the operation of constitutionalizing fascism succeeded in terms of the movement in its entirety, it failed with regard to what the regime proved to be. Notwithstanding all the compromises that fascism had to make with the old ruling class and the political personnel of the regime, in the course of ten years fascism had achieved a virtual monopoly of power, and the old political ruling class that made the compromise with fascism in 1922 was almost entirely excluded. If the war had not brought about the fall of the regime in 1943, this process would have become ever greater and would have established graver difficulties for those centers of effective power that were still in the hands of the old ruling class at that time. I am referring in particular to the crown, to the army, and to a lesser extent the judiciary. That is to say, to the centers of power that fascism—given the character of compromise of its success—had dominated only marginally.

Roughly the same thing can be said about the Catholic world. The events that followed the fall of fascism should not be permitted to deceive us: Without the defeat, the Catholic world as well would have been slowly eroded by fascism. The crisis of 1931 is significant: It shows well that the Catholic sector was becoming de-Catholicized and nationalized. The great postwar success of the Christian Democratic party was due above all to two facts: The role that the Church had had during the last phase of the war (remember what Chabod has to say about this)[26] and even more, the moderate, anticommunist, and modern face that the Christian Democrats were able to put on at that time.

4
Italian Fascism: Historical and Comparative Analysis

Ledeen: What do you think about the relationship between fascism, which followed on the heels of World War I, and the political forces of prefascist society? I would specifically like to hear what you have to say about the thesis according to which fascism was a movement for the defense of traditional Italy, or of the industrial class against the presumed revolutionary menace from the Left. Who made the fascist rise to power easier, aside from the strategy of Giolitti and *trasformismo*? How did the fascists manage to arrive at the seat of power in Italy?

De Felice: Fascism was unconsciously helped by almost all the political forces of the liberal, democratic type. However, this was not done in an active, deliberate manner. They were helped, for example, in 1922, when they arrived in the government, by the idea that fascism could be constitutionalized and deradicalized simply by making space for it in the government. That was so because nobody had truly recognized the character of fascism and the profound innovation it represented. They dealt with fascism as they had with the other political forces.

In the first period, in 1919 and 1920 up until the end of "the great fear" of the occupation of factories and the events of Palazzo d'Accursio and Castello Estense, fascism was not taken seriously by anyone and it had had no major role in the political life of the country. That was true because it was weak, ambiguous, and because its programs and leaders were considered extremists and subversive. In the next phase, from the end of 1920 to mid-1922 (up until the failure of the so-called Sciopero legalitario), things changed.

Fascism had its greatest success in agrarian zones, especially where the system of leagues and the organizations of farm workers were strongest. Fascism obtained economic support from agrarian forces there. This picture is much less true in the industrial and financial world of the cities. Here, too, fascism found supporters and help, even substantial help. But this aid was of a highly personal nature: The squads were financed so that they might reestablish local order, drive the red and white trade-union organizations into crisis, and prevent strikes. But this is not a general phenomenon and it concerns primarily medium-sized and small industrialists. It was the small industries—who found themselves in the greatest economic difficulties; who had fewer reserves and a smaller capacity to contract—that looked to fascism. Large industry did it much less. There was even money from the large industrialists; we have the evidence. However, it was not a question of large sums, but rather money given sporadically to avoid trouble in the factories. The small industrialists wanted to be supported and helped; the large ones desired above all that the fascists not create disorder that would aggravate the situation in the factories, and they paid them off, satisfying to some extent the fascist request for economic support.

It is unthinkable that Italy's great economic forces wanted to bring fascism to power. Fascism for them was a "white guard" that would be sent home once its task had been accomplished. It is difficult to challenge the thesis that the Italian economic world in 1922 behaved as the political world; it also wanted to insert fascism into the government to weaken and constitutionalize it. The industrialists certainly had no thought of giving fascism exclusive power. In 1922 the economic world was thinking of solutions with Giolitti, Orlando, or above all with Salandra. The fascists would have collaborated with such a government, but they would have occupied a subordinate position. They arrived at the point where they hoped to form a government with Salandra at the head and Mussolini as minister of the interior. This meant not only that fascism had to be constitutionalized and emasculated, but also that if the squads had provoked disorders it would have been Mussolini himself who would have had to discipline them. Here we have the proof of a total lack of realism and a singular political impotence, but it confirms what I said before: The economic world behaved like the political world; it nurtured the same hopes and the same projects.

The real knot to be untied in understanding how fascism reached power is not that of the attitude of the economic world toward fascism, but that of the mass base of fascism in 1921 and 1922, both at the level of its adherents and of public opinion.

In order to arrive at a historical understanding, it is not so important to establish the degree to which fascism was dependent on certain forces of interests as it is to understand the extent to which and why it was autonomous of them. Only in this manner is it possible to evaluate the causes of the errors of the traditional ruling class. We must analyze the novelty of fascism and its success, both at the mass level and at the political level, properly speaking.

Ledeen: Can we turn now to the regime? In your last book, *Mussolini the Duce*, you spoke of a regime and a country fundamentally in agreement with Mussolini—the famous consensus. But at the same time that you speak of consensus, you speak of a Mussolini who viewed the real triumph of fascism in a rather distant future in which Italy was to have been truly fascisticized. If this is true, is it possible to speak about a paradoxical failure of fascism precisely at the moment of its greatest success, when it reached this great national consensus? It had failed in achieving its vision of the Italian future. And if it is possible to speak of a failure of fascism during the years of consensus, what is the nature of this failure? What is the connection between this failure and what followed? To put it somewhat differently, what constitutes what you have called the true and only crisis of the regime, the contradiction within fascism that made it impossible to create that new ruling class that alone would have permitted Mussolini to perpetuate fascism in the new generation and to project it toward the future?

De Felice: This is all a single problem, a problem connected with the kind of fascistization undertaken in these years of greatest consensus, 1929 to 1936. The consensus of these years is a consensus for a certain Italian situation; in part an economic one, in part a social peace that must be linked not only to the Italian situation but also to the much more serious crisis of France and England in these years, not to mention that of Germany and the United States. The consensus stems from the contrast between different situations and different realities. The country was thinking more about the evils that fascism had avoided than whether it brought true benefits. The consensus was based on that which Italy did *not* have, on the disadvantages that had been avoided, on the security of life that, for better or for worse, fascism had guaranteed to Italians. Then there is the Western foreign policy, which Mussolini followed at least until 1934, and which appeared to be a peaceful one.

Ledeen: In short, fascism was essentially conceived as a system of national defense.

De Felice: Fascism was conceived as an instrument to avoid difficulties on an international scale for the country. With the major powers, fascism presented itself as a peaceful regime, a regime that did not hear the siren's call of the Führer when Hitler came to power; on the contrary, it opposed him. At the beginning, the Ethiopian war itself (and I believe I have demonstrated this in my biography of Mussolini) was viewed with anxiety, because it was thought that the war might bring about difficulties with England and France. The war with Ethiopia generated an enthusiastic consensus, a moment of national excitement, but only when it was clear that the English and the French were not moving, and that Italy was conquering its empire.

Here again, we must be careful: The Italian nationalism behind the Ethiopian war, the mass nationalism, is not of the classic, materialistic sort. It is rather a populist one, and contains a strong dose of elements that come from a certain "southernism." It is not an imperialism of the French or English type. It is an imperialism, a colonialism based on immigration, which hoped that large numbers of Italians would be able to transfer into new territories to find work, to find opportunities that they did not have in their native land. In short, one does not leave so much with the idea of exploiting the colonies, as with the hope of being able to find land and work.

All of this—together with many other causes that I have indicated in my last volume—explains the consensus, but it gives it some extremely precarious characteristics. When the economic situation became more difficult, when the intervention in the Spanish civil war and, above all, the creation of the Axis occurred (an alliance that was absolutely unpopular among the great majority of Italians—with all the consequences that this brought, the racial campaign, and so on), when, in other words, the sense of security weakened and the hopes of a few years before disappeared, the consensus became ever weaker. This does not mean that it was not recuperable. If Mussolini had kept Italy out of World War II, he would have reacquired a great part of the lost consensus. Perhaps it would have become even stronger. The enthusiasm for Mussolini on the day of the Munich Conference is a significant fact. But it is unthinkable that Mussolini could have remained outside the war.

Ledeen: Let us leave the discussion of the war for later.

De Felice: All of this brings us to another sort of consideration: Mussolini understood the precariousness of this kind of consensus; the Duce was not as stupid as many people would have us believe, and he had a great gift for understanding the masses. He understood perfectly the conditioning of the consensus; indeed, he did not trust it, even if he had to come to terms with it for the moment. This is the source of his lack of faith in the Italians. He was beleaguered by the necessity of having to administer them day by day with demogogic initiative and other techniques ranging from personal concessions to the use of terror and police control.

From here as well stems the necessity of establishing his own future on the basis of a vision of a completely different type of man; given that this kind of consensus was the only base permitted him to remain in power, it was necessary to create a new kind of Italian in the new generations, a type that would be different from that with which he had to deal at that moment.

Here we come to an extremely interesting question. The idea that the state could create a new kind of citizen through education was a typically democratic idea. It was indeed a classic idea of the Enlightenment, a manifestation of a Rousseauian character. If we read the *Plot of Babeuf*,[27] for example, we see that this is one of the central points in the Babeuvist program (and not just the Babeuvists: it is all an Enlightenment mentality, Rousseauian, Blanquist, Proudhonian). This is very significant, because the cultural roots of this Mussolinian concept are typical of the ideas of his youth, which was linked to a left-wing radicalism (and not a right-wing radicalism, to which nazism was linked).

Ledeen: Let us try to analyze this concept, which seems to me rather new, especially for the Italian reader.

De Felice: Yes, because it is not a great discovery for Anglo-Saxon culture.

Ledeen: Perhaps it is worth the trouble to clarify our discussion at this point. We are confronted with an attempt to bring the Italian masses under control, putting the emphasis on the action of the fascist government more in the sphere of human behavior and human sentiment than in that of social institutions. Irving Louis Horowitz,[28] writing about Sorel, has called this ideology "the concept of will opposed to that of organization, as purity of conviction opposes a suffocating rationalism." This ideology can easily be found both in Mussolini's speeches and in the articles of fascist "believers" during the period of Mussolini's rule.

If we keep in mind that the fascist revolution was based on the creation of new human beings and that it was necessary to wait for their arrival in order to create truly fascist institutions,[29] we shall better understand the characteristics of these institutions and their virtual lack of structure. It may seem paradoxical, but the failure of fascist social policy is the direct consequence of the theory of the fascist revolution, according to which the fulfillment of the revolution could take place only in a future period, when Italy would be populated by fascist citizens psychologically and morally different from the existing Italians.

De Felice: It is an idea based on the concept of progress, and therefore we find ourselves on a terrain completely different from that on which the analysis of fascism is generally conducted.

Ledeen: While the nazis wanted to eliminate the progress of the last two centuries and to clear the ground of the achievements of the industrial revolution, of capitalism, and of urbanism, the fascists wanted to do something completely new.

De Felice: There is a ruralistic component, a polemic against urbanism and superindustrialism in fascism as well. However, it fits into a petit bourgeois-democratic tradition.

Ledeen: Both nazism and Italian fascism saw a grave menace in the great cities, a menace against the spirit of the people, and therefore an enemy of fascist progress.

De Felice: I am not a specialist of these issues, however I have the impression that the same kind of hostility toward urbanism (not for heavy industry) is strongly felt in the Soviet Union as well.

Ledeen: Then there is the famous introduction of Mussolini to Korherr's book[30] that speaks of the drop of the birthrate signifying the death of peoples. I am thinking particularly of the point at which he talks about the danger of the sterilization of the Italian people, if everyone comes to live in the big cities. This concept represents the search for a new kind of fascist man who is vital, virile, strong, and independent, full of imagination and energy.

De Felice: And who is frugal? This is an important fact: In Mussolini's time the problems of consumerism did not exist for Italy. However, consumerism could never have been part of Mussolini's conception. He stressed frugality for the population (and not just for practical motives) because to him it was a moral virtue.

Ledeen: During the years of the consensus, Italians were certainly not what Mussolini wanted.

De Felice: From this point of view, one can understand his unhappiness with the Italians.

Ledeen: At the height of his fortune, the transformation of the Italian people had barely begun. Mussolini
required far more profound fascistization. What was
the means of this transformation? Education, all by
itself, or were there other systems?

De Felice: Education was a positive element. Then
there was a long series of repressive measures, destined for those people who departed from "standard"
behavior (in Mussolini's logic). The real problem, although we must judge on the basis of a limited period
(long periods—probably several generations—are
required for the transformation of a people through
education), was that the results among the new generations were undoubtedly unsatisfactory. This is
linked to something I wrote in my last volume, that
the failure of fascism lies in its incapacity to give life
to a new ruling class that would substitute for the one
in power. As you have written,[31] Mussolini favored
the new generation. The publications of Italian youth
enjoyed a greater liberty than the others; young Italians had more opportunity than adults for their de-
bates, and so on. However, notwithstanding this form
of liberalism with regard to youth, the fundamental
notion remains: They would all be formed according
to a preconceived idea, without allowing them the
possibility of developing freely, even in the context of
fascist logic.

The crisis with the Holy See over Azione Cattolica
is very important in this context. The crisis of 1931
was determined by the necessity that fascism maintain a monopoly over the formation of Italian youth.
This constant preoccupation was felt not only among
the ruling circles of fascism (which was contrary to
any liberalization), but by Mussolini as well. It is
typical—and this is one of the gravest of his errors—

that when the Duce launched the operations in East Africa, he blocked every form of internal debate among youth. He had always said that youth must discuss, must talk.

Ledeen: "Make way for youth."

De Felice: "Make way for youth," precisely. Mussolini had advocated special treatment for youth, but when the war began, everything was reduced to "believe, obey, fight." This was principally a question of face, to give the impression of a monolithic country. But it was also that Mussolini had a charismatic vision of his own power. Everyone must submerge themselves in his policies, his personality. They must be participants in the Mussolinian myth, because only his myth was capable of holding things intact in difficult moments.

This was a symptom of a grave lack of faith in both the old and the young generations, who were excluded from every active, responsible, and thoughtful participation in the great problems of the African war. After all, the Ethiopian question was not only one of waging war, but also principally one of creating the new fascism after the conquest of the empire. What little had been obtained in the past was rendered vain. A profound sense of lack of confidence was created, which then worsened with the Spanish civil war and the policy toward Germany. All of this contributed to make the crisis of the new generations even more serious, both quantatively and, above all, for its repercussions on fascist policy and on the more general crisis of the regime itself.

Ledeen: If the failure of fascism—which you have called the "crisis of the regime"—was due to internal

causes, how do you explain the fact that the crisis of
fascism has almost always been discussed in terms of
foreign policy? Everyone has said that if Mussolini
had not entered World War II and lost, fascism would
have lasted.

De Felice: Fascism would have lasted longer if he
had not entered the war. But he could not fail to enter
it, because one could ask anything of Mussolini ex-
cept neutrality (it is easier to imagine him entering
the war against Germany than it is to imagine him
remaining neutral). But if the war brought about the
fall of fascism, this does not mean that what we said
earlier is not valid. Even if it had not fallen, fascism
would have been transformed in any event—in un-
foreseeable ways—and would not have evolved in the
sense that Mussolini thought. To understand this
better, as a purely hypothetical question, we can
think about the evolution that Franco's regime in
Spain had undergone in the last thirty years. You
may say that this regime had undergone a slow
liberalization, a passing away of certain ideas of earlier times, because it found itself isolated after the
fall of its German and Italian allies.

Ledeen: In my opinion, Franco's regime was not fascist.

De Felice: It was not, and we might well discuss if it
ever was. More probably it was a classic authoritarian regime with certain modern elements, but nothing more. In any event, it is not Franco who interests
us now, but rather the fact that fascism would have
undergone a revolution that would have had to come
to terms with an extremely important event—the
death of Mussolini. Depending on the circumstances

in which this took place, his death would undoubtedly have produced grave repercussions on the fascists. It could have offered the opportunity to recuperate some strength to the old ruling class, gathered around the monarchy, thanks to the explosion of struggles for the succession that might have been grave enough to weaken the regime. Alternatively, it could have put new tendencies in motion, which would surely have developed—if the regime had continued to live—from that critical and discontented fascism of the new generation that had come to maturity in the meantime. Mussolini's death would have been an extremely dramatic event especially if it were not preceded by his withdrawal from the government by an indirect control of power through his successor. But it would not have been sufficient to produce the fall of the regime itself.

With all of its negative aspects, fascism had one positive aspect, even if it was so only in part due to fascism itself, and much more a merit of the objective development of a modern or semimodern society in Italy in those years. Fascism as regime, albeit slowly and in far more distorted forms than fascism as movement would have wished, had developed the first level of a new ruling class. Through the institutions of the regime a new political context was being created—administrative, syndical, and technical— that brought together the characteristics of a very recent social promotion (in part a result of fascism) and of a new participation through the channels of the regime. This new ruling class that was slowly being formed—certain studies of Farneti,[32] in part unfinished and unpublished, anticipated by him in speeches for international congresses, demonstrate it—would not have passively accepted a return in force by the old ruling class. This is true even if this new ruling class were fascist (in the Mussolinian sense) only extremely superficially. A liberal evolution would therefore have occurred. There was also the possibility of a succession, which could have lead to a different solution. I am not referring to any one person in particular, but to the conception of fascism that Dino Grandi (among others) had of fascism: That is, of fascists who believed that fascism had fulfilled its role for some time, and that therefore one must arrive at a more centralized and less democratic regime than the prefascist one, but more constitutional than fascism. In short, an intermediary stage between the two. This would have meant precious little, if we look at it from the present standpoint, but a great deal if we consider the reality of the period.

Ledeen: We have spoken of the consensus; we have talked about the strength of the fascist regime; we have talked about the possible lines of development that fascism might have taken after the death of Mussolini. But we have not spoken about the technique of manipulation of the masses by fascism—and thus far you have not written about this in your biography of Mussolini. At the present moment of fascist revival, this subject has become exceedingly contemporary and important. What importance did the technique of mass manipulation have? Was it important in the creation of a consensus around the regime or was it simply a kind of comic opera, a spectacle Italian style?

De Felice: I do not believe that one can speak of a comic opera. In all discussions of the technique of fascist power, especially for the part that concerns Mussolini himself, there is a very precise conception of the masses, of the crowds, that the Duce inherited from Sorel and principally from Le Bon, which he sought to enact. Mussolini was convinced that the charismatic function of his power had to be expressed through a dialogue with the people. In short, the leader gives the word of order, the enthusiasm, and mobilizes the energies of the people around him. It is the classic concept of charisma. However, this is not the crucial point of the technique of fascist power.

The major point is represented by the control of the instruments of mass information. The balcony address was simply the culminating moment, the moment of enthusiasm, the fusion of the masses with the leader—or at least he wished that it were so; and it was on several occasions. This is only one of the aspects of the system. The basic discussion of fascism must be developed around the control that fascism exercised over all forms of information, and therefore on the enormous importance assumed not only by the traditional instruments of information (the press), but even more by the movies and radio—true vehicles of mass information. One must add the very important element of the school, on all levels, from elementary school to the university. It is all a mosaic, and one cannot give one element more importance than another; even if fascism obtained its most spectacular successes through charismatic action by Mussolini, one could still not explain the consensus without the entire mosaic.

Fascist mass policy became the fulcrum of the fascist system—trade unions had an important role that Togliatti saw well[33]—along with a series of social, recreational, and sporting initiatives—because for fascism the consensus and participation of the masses in the regime had to be active. For fascism it was necessary that the masses feel mobilized and integrated into the regime, both because they had a direct relationship with the charismatic leader, and because they were participants in a revolutionary process. This revolutionary process was supposed to create a new moral community in Italy, with its own ideals, models of behavior (for example, the use of the "*voi*" instead of "*lei*") and hierarchy. The creation of this community awaited the new generations, but it is extremely important to stress that this was the only way in which the regime could become a legitimate power that would no longer have to use coercion to assert its authority. Had fascism succeeded in creating this desired moral community, this political power would have become increasingly autonomous and prevalent compared to that (in large part economic) still firmly in the hands of the flankers.

It is very difficult to speak of ritual. Ritual existed—the salute to the Duce, the call to the fallen heroes—but it does not have a decisive role. Here we have another difference with Germany, where ritual tends to become everything. Everything has a place in the ritual, understood in its many aspects, to the point where Hitler himself did not want to be thought of as a charismatic figure, but rather as an integral aspect of the ritual itself. This is explained very well by Mosse[34]: Hitler had a tremendous charismatic charge, but his successors for the "millennium" did not. Since this weakening of charismatic charge from the Führer to his successors might produce imbalances within the regime and bring about unexpected difficulties, Hitler forced himself to depersonalize his own figure in order to integrate it into the ritual and become an inseparable part of it. In this way he hoped that the day when the Führer would no longer be Adolph Hitler, the difference would not be noticed and the nazi regime would not have to undergo any unexpected changes.

Ledeen: Let us return to Italian fascism. Given that Mussolini had absolute control of all the means of

information and all the fascist organizations such as
the Ballilla, how was it that he failed in his intention
of transforming the Italian people? How was it that
he did not succeed in producing the new fascist man,
having every possibility to achieve it in his hands?

De Felice: He had all the instruments in his hands,
but the instruments are nothing if there are not men
who are able to use them. The case of the school seems
typical. The instrument of the school was completely
in the hands of the regime; however, the functioning
of that instrument passed through the hands of
teachers at various levels. Until new teachers were
created by fascism, it was necessary to use the older
generation, and in this manner the old problem of the
chicken and the egg presents itself.

Ledeen: I agree. And the same thing can be said
about fascist syndicalism. In the relationship, for
example, between industrialists and workers, one
finds always the same language and the same protest
on the part of industrialists: The workers were not yet
fascisticized, they had not been transformed at the
roots. On the other hand, when Bottai was minister of
corporations he frequently complained about the old
mentality of the industrialists, who kept on putting
blocks in the way of his efforts to exercise greater
control over their operations. Can it be said that
while an ideology for the fascistization of the masses
(and perhaps also for certain groups higher up)
existed, fascism failed because the old ruling class did
not collaborate? Or is there perhaps some other fundamental element that was lacking in the fascist
vision?

De Felice: Fascism did not use the instruments that
it had in its hands with sufficient efficacy because

there was a great deal lacking at the level of cultural groups and of humanistic formation. At the level of the formation of groups of technical culture, on the other hand, fascism had excellent technicians (who in many cases were not true fascists). Given their mentality, the technicians—who believed that their work was apolitical—ended up by becoming among the most important executors of the politics of the regime.

Ledeen: The old dream of Massimo Rocca.

De Felice: Yes, at the technical level. These technicians had even the majority of the *comités d'état* that fascism had had were not fascists, neither from the ideological point of view nor from that of membership in the party. One's mind turns immediately to men such as Serpieri Beneduce, Osio, and many others. But then we forget how many of these technicians were lost to fascism in 1938 and 1939. To take the world of physics, for example, think about Fermi. What would have happened to Fermi without the anti-Semitic legislation?

Ledeen: He would have remained an Italian physicist . . .

De Felice: . . .who was not interested in politics. The greatest failure of the regime took place in the field of humanistic culture. One could undertake a very long discussion on this point and see if these humanists were different from the technicians, and analyze the influences upon them before and during fascism. It is too broad a question to deal with here, without undertaking—and this would be absolutely indispensable—a long analysis of Italian culture in those years.

5
Fascism, Foreign Policy, and World War II

Ledeen: To return to the consensus, what are the ties between it and Mussolini's foreign policy?

De Felice: This is a very complicated matter, which I have treated in my most recent volume on the years of consensus. Given the nature of the regime and relations between the components of the international situation (especially after Hitler's arrival in power), the desire on the part of Mussolini and many fascist leaders to undertake a revivification and further enlargement of fascism could not be based solely on domestic policy. Once the attempt to fascisticize the Italian people in the late twenties and the early thirties had failed, fascism attempted to become progressively more totalitarian and to reduce the period necessary for fascisticizing the masses to a minimum. In this attempt it turned to foreign policy. Foreign policy becomes increasingly the keystone of fascist policy beginning with the Ethiopian war. Only in this way—to return to our discussion on consensus— could fascism have won its contest with the traditional ruling class. If it had arrived at the decisive moment of "after Mussolini" with its *own* charisma,

the traditional ruling class would have had very slim
possibilities of recapturing power.

Ledeen: We come, then, to the war and we must take
a look at the Axis, the alliance with Hitler. Was the
alliance with Hitler a part of the internal logic of
Italian fascism? In what sense was the Axis inevitable?

De Felice: To base one's analysis on the theory that
the alliance was inevitable would be a gross error.
Many maintain that the alliance was inevitable,
simply because these were two regimes with certain
points in common—very many in the opinion of some,
but I disagree with theories of the identity of the two
regimes. From an ideological point of view, the alliance was not inevitable at all. It became so for
reasons of a political nature. Fest[35] is also of this
opinion, and he is the finest biographer of Hitler. In
passing, however, it should be noted that to say as he
does that the African war had made the alliance
inevitable, anticipates the question a great deal.
After the African expedition, Mussolini had no idea
whatsoever of a pact with Hitler. This does not mean
that the alliance was not a consequence of the fact
that, with the Ethiopian war, Mussolini's foreign policy entered a crisis. His idea to go into Africa with the
backing of the English and French was a failure;
moreover, the Popular Front had arrived in power in
France, which meant, at least for the moment, that
all hopes for a pact between Rome and Paris were
dashed.

Mussolini was faced with the necessity of finding a
new formula of international relations that did not
isolate Italy. After the African war, he prolonged the
formula of the "pendulum" policy—the oscillation between Germany and England—the so-called policy of

the "determinant weight." In the new situation, however, the possibilities of realizing this strategy of the pendulum became increasingly limited. The Spanish civil war threatened this policy even more, because the attitude of many countries with regard to Italian fascism became increasingly ideological. Their antifascism—which had existed before and had become even more intense, but which had never been a determinant at the level of the governments—then became determinant in the case of the French government, while the international antifascist camp became larger. From this situation stemmed the great difficulties of the policy of the pendulum: Mussolini continued to effect it, but the arc of the pendulum became narrower and narrower.

Despite the necessity of injecting an ever-greater ideological charge into fascist policy in the new climate (a climate that lead Mussolini inevitably to established ideological and contingent ties with nazism), Mussolini remained suspicious and fearful of the ever-growing German aggressiveness. This problem is extremely complicated and requires further research and study; however, I do not believe that one can say with absolute certainty that Mussolini did not enter the war in 1939 solely because he was unprepared or because he was irritated at having been tricked by Hitler. The Führer had led him to believe—indeed had said so explicitly—that there would be no war prior to 1943, while he had instead precipitated it in 1939. Mussolini was probably still uncertain and fearful about the international and military situation, but there was also a residue of distrust for Germany. He decided to intervene only in 1940—and by then German victory seemed inevitable.

Entering the war meant, on the one hand, not acting the part of someone who defends certain positions and then does not follow through with the consequences; on the other hand, it meant guaranteeing that Italy would have the possibility of playing the role of a major power. Mussolini was afraid that Germany might feel betrayed for a second time by Italian bad faith. Betrayed in 1914, betrayed again in 1939. He was also terrified of the possibility that Germany, by then clear master of the field—having beaten France and evidently about to defeat England— might turn its endeavors against Italy. It was not necessary that these endeavors be military and territorial in nature. At that moment it could well have been a simple vendetta of disqualifying Italy from the upper strata of the hierarchy of nations. Mussolini was well aware—Italian documents that demonstrate this have been published—that his intervention in France would have an extremely negative impression on international public opinion: "They will accuse us of stabbing France in the back." Given the way things were going, once he had decided to intervene Mussolini would have preferred to enter the war even earlier than he actually did. It was Hitler who attempted to delay the Italian entry at this point. The Duce was in a hurry, he was afraid of public opinion, he wanted to attack a wounded man who was still on his feet, not a dying man. This is another reason why I do not believe that the alliance between Italy and Germany stemmed essentially from a presumed affinity or, even worse, an ideological identity of the two regimes. The Axis originated instead from a certain kind of policy that both nazism and fascism enacted and that, willfully in the first case and gradually as the possibilities of carrying through the policy of the pendulum vanished in the second case, in the end carried Germany and Italy into the same camp. This may appear to be a subtle distinction, but it must be kept in mind.

Ledeen: That is to say it was not an ideological alliance.

De Felice: It was not an ideological alliance; or at least the ideology existed above all as a negative fact.

Ledeen: In what sense a negative fact?

De Felice: In the sense that they had common enemies and that these became increasingly numerous.

Ledeen: Are these not ideological enemies?

De Felice: Yes, above all, communism; and then democracy as well. But for Hitler, hatred for democracy and the democratic states was all of a piece, while for Mussolini, who believed in the idea of progress (and hoped, at least at the beginning, that all of Europe would become fascist) and above all feared the dynamism and hegemony of the Germans, the ideological and the political problem remained separate and distinct for a long time. This does not mean that the ideals in these ideologies were the same. The societies that the two regimes wished to bring into existence were exceedingly different.

Ledeen: In what sense then would you say that World War II was an ideological war, a war between fascism and antifascism, between fascism and democracy?

De Felice: There is much to be analyzed at various levels. At the level of various governments, of the ruling classes, and of the masses, the differences are fairly evident. World War II became an ideological war gradually, but at the beginning the ideological elements, although they were present, were not determinant. You are an American. Let us then take as an example American public opinion: If America felt ideologically involved in the war, why was it so difficult to accept the war itself, and why did they consider Japan to be its greatest enemy instead of Germany? In the scale of enemies, first came the Japanese, then the Germans. Perhaps because the latter were more distant, because the war with them could be avoided or delayed, while Japan represented a more immediate menace. But was it only this? Had the war been an ideological one, this would not be sufficient to explain the matter. The pacifist element in the United States was so strong that it has even been suggested that Roosevelt knew about the Japanese attack against Pearl Harbor before it took place, and that he did nothing to prevent it because he believed that only in this manner could the United States be brought into the war. This greatly weakens the hypothesis that the war was, at least for the United States, a question of ideology. To say that there were groups, even numerous and powerful ones, in the United States who considered the European war ideological and who therefore wanted to enter, is one thing; but to say that the United States felt the war to be ideological seems excessive. With the passage of time this changed because there was an escalation in the manipulation of the masses. A great propaganda machine was put into action that pushed the country onto the road of ideologizing the conflict.

Ledeen: In both America and England there is a commonplace about democracies and war: In order to wage war effectively, a democracy must wage a total war. Limited, tactical wars are extremely difficult for democratic forms of government. When America entered World War II, it put all of its energies to work. It was a total war. There is also another factor: The Japanese attack against the United States at Pearl Harbor—given the existence of the alliance between Japan, Germany, and Italy—was simultaneously an attack by the Germans and Italians. Thus, if the war were to be waged, it had to be waged on both fronts. In any event, I agree with you. It is extremely difficult to defend the thesis that a great wave of public opinion drove the United States into this antifascist war. Many American historians maintain—and I am about eighty percent in agreement with them—that without the Japanese attack, America probably would not have entered the war in time to have had a determinent effect.

De Felice: There was another important fact: The war became ideological only after the German attack on the Soviet Union. Up until that moment, an important element of Western public opinion—that part controlled by the communist parties—had an extremely ambiguous attitude toward the war, which made it more difficult for the war to assume an ideological character. The war became ideological when the fascist states were completely isolated, and when the Soviet Union passed into the opposing camp. The French and English governments conducted secret negotiations in 1939 attempting to resolve the conflict. If they were thinking about the possibility of ending the war at the peace table instead of conquering their enemies on the battlefield, the war could not have had an ideological character. An ideological war by its very nature must end with the extermination of the opponents. The character of the alliance between Germany and the Soviet Union

made it more difficult to give an ideological significance to the war.

Ledeen: Given the fascist and nazi ideologies, does it
not seem extremely probable, if not inevitable, that
on the fascist side war would be waged against democracy and communism, and that therefore the di-
vision between the two sides would have been
ideological? The alliance between Germany and Italy
is a rather natural one, both politically and ideologically, and it seems that the opposing alliance between
Russia, France, and England was also natural. Do
you agree? Was the antifascist alliance based on its
own logic?

De Felice: The antifascist alliance had this logic, but
I do not know whether it had it at the beginning of the
conflict. The fact that Englishmen and Frenchmen,
in the winter of 1939-40, thought very seriously indeed, and then decided—even if the actual enactment
was delayed for technical motives—upon armed intervention against the Soviet Union on behalf of Fin-
land (which would have inevitably meant dragging
the Soviets into battle on the side of Germany given
the alliance between Berlin and Moscow) demon-
strates that the ideological character of the conflict
was rather weak, and that it was not considered impossible that the Hitler-Stalin pact might last, and
was not destined to be destroyed by one of the two
partners. There is even more: Hitler said that the
outcome of the war would be determined by Japan,
when the anti-American forces gained the upper
hand over the anti-Soviet forces in Japan. After what
we have said about the attitude of the United States,
this raises another fascinating question: If Pearl
Harbor was necessary for America to enter into war,

if the Americans had not been attacked by the Japanese, had the Japanese—as Hitler wished—directed their attack not beyond the seas but on the continent, against the Soviet Union, what would have been the reaction of America?

Ledeen: Who knows? Asia has always been very important for American foreign policy. In a sense it has been more important than Europe, and a threat of Japanese expansion on the Asian continent would have been very serious for the United States. Sooner or later America would have entered the war.

De Felice: But not for ideological motives; for motives of power.

Ledeen: Yes, traditional American motives, imperialistic ones. For America it was necessary to sustain the famous policy of the "open door" in the Orient, keeping Asia open to American commerce, American industry, and American expansion in general. It was a principle of fundamental importance.

De Felice: Let us return to the discussion we were having earlier. I think we agree on the fundamental points. World War II became the greatest ideological war in history only bit by bit. The intensity of this war was not foreseeable at the beginning of the conflict; the ideological component became decisive only after the German attack against the Soviet Union.

Ledeen: I have one final question in this regard. You once said that Mussolini gave a very important talk to his generals in the winter of 1939 in which he said roughly that the western frontier and the eastern frontier had been secured, and it was necessary to secure the northern front. It was a speech from which one might imply that he did not exclude the possibility of complications with Germany.

De Felice: This is further confirmation of what I said earlier: Mussolini did not intervene in 1939 not only because he was unprepared or because he was angry with Hitler, but also because he had not made a final decision of sides. Mussolini could not—with all his demogogic ability and with all the control of mass media—change public opinion. He could not deny what he had said up until then and play a neutral role.

Ledeen: Also because by then he had proclaimed that fascism had become universal.

De Felice: The universality of fascism, in that logic, did not permit neutrality. Perhaps Mussolini's uncertainties were due to a form of timidity and suspicion with regard to Hitler. This suspicion grew after the pact with Russia, which was extremely unpopular both at the level of the fascist ruling class and among Italian public opinion.

6
True Examples of Fascism

Ledeen: We have spoken about Italian fascism and a bit on German nazism. Let us now talk about fascism in general. In *Interpretations of Fascism* you said that the social base of fascism—that is, the middle classes—must be kept in mind to understand the phenomenon. You say that fascism must be analyzed in the context of the more-or-less industrialized countries of Western Europe between the two world wars. How do you respond to those who, like Weber,[36] for example, speak of a primitive fascism in Rumania, where there were no middle classes; or to those who, like Gregor,[37] speak of fascism outside the European context, of Arab fascism like Nasser's movement or Qadaffi's. Is fascism necessarily the creation of the middle classes of industrialized countries?

De Felice: I am very insistent that fascism is a phenomenon that must be rigidly limited, otherwise we shall not understand anything. It must be limited chronologically, between the two world wars. It must be limited geographically, to Western Europe, that is to say, that part of Europe that had undergone a process of liberalization and democratization. Finally it must be limited from the social point of view. Fascism, in its emergence and affirmation, is a phenomenon of the middle classes.

Those who speak of fascism with regard to Libya and Egypt—there are those who have spoken about other countries of the Third World and also Perónism in Argentina—are mistaken (even for Perónism, which is apparently most similar to European fascism). If we undertake this analysis in modern scientific terms (for example, the analysis of various kinds of mobilization, and the more specific categories of Gino Germani in his most recent article)[38] one cannot call these regimes fascist, at least with the meaning of the historical experiences that this word summarizes.

Insofar as Rumania is concerned, aside from the fact that I believe it would be better to talk about fascisms in power apart from those that did not arrive in power, there is an abyss between Codreanu and Antonescu. To limit the discussion to Codreanu, it is difficult in his case to speak of fascism in the true sense of the word. At the very least, the fascist components of his movement are the least significant, the least characteristic. It would be better to talk about populism in this case. There are populist elements in fascism as well, but it is a matter of establishing the relative importance of the various ingredients. The populist components in fascism are few and far between, as are the fascist components of Codreanu's movement. This discussion could carry us far afield, and perhaps we can take it up again later on, because it is not an accident that Codreanu today has had great success among groups of the extreme Right: A success far greater than Mussolini's. And this must make us think: These groups who invoked the name of Codreanu did not invoke the name of Mussolini.

Ledeen: I have a somewhat different comparison in mind between these two movements. While I agree with you in large part, I think we must recognize that during the thirties the fascists themselves thought that Codreanu's movement was fascist. When Italian fascists spoke of other fascisms, they were skeptical about many of these; for example, the Spanish Falangist movement of José Antonio Primo de Rivera was greatly discussed. Some thought that it was fascist, others that it was not. But on Codreanu they all agreed; his was a true fascist movement, and indeed they gave him a great amount of money.

De Felice: Money does not mean anything. They gave money, for example, to the Austrian Heimwehren, which was certainly not fascist. I do not think that Prince Starhemberg can be considered fascist. Giving money means nothing, because at a given moment certain forces were important to the game, and were therefore aided and abetted. Primo de Rivera is much closer to an ideal type of fascism (which I do not believe exists) than Codreanu.

Ledeen: I think so, too, but the fact remains . . .

De Felice: . . . that a certain kind of relationship (and certain intermediaries) existed between Rumania and Italy, such that the position of Codreanu was overrated, while the scarcity of relations between Rome and Primo de Rivera led to his being underrated. I have grave doubts about the fruitfulness of this kind of research on the "quantum" of pure fascism, on the minimum or the maximum, as if one could weigh these movements on some kind of ideological scale and then give them a label. There is a danger of ending up by enrolling all of them in the fascist world, of ending with Nolte's theory,[39] as, for

example, when he lists even the Action Francaise in
the ranks of fascism, which is absolutely impossible
from any point of view.

Ledeen: What sense do you think Nolte's definition
of the fascist epoch has?[40]

De Felice: If we take this concept in the sense that
Nolte intended it and that of his closest followers
(there are very few of them but—with very few
exceptions—they are harmful), in the rigid sense,
then I think it has no importance at all. If on the other
hand we take it in a somewhat tangential sense, then
it has a certain value, especially if it refers to Europe.
Let us leave people like Chandra Bose and others,
who have nothing to do with fascism, otherwise we
shall end up putting all the anti-English and anti-
French movements in the fascist camp and then
Ghandi and Bourgiba become fascists. When one
speaks of Europe between the two wars, meaning by
this a period of general crisis that takes a certain
consistency especially after the economic crash of
1929, and becomes a moral and political crisis that
spreads to vast sectors of the bourgeoisie and certain
intellectual circles. It is a crisis of confidence with
regard to democracy and capitalism—in their effi-
ciency and functionality—which then becomes larger
and spreads to broad elements of society. In this situation there is a revival of interest in those experiences considered to be alternatives to democracy, and
there is an attempt to put an end to the main dysfunc-
tions of capitalism. There is a great interest in attack-
ing democracy and capitalism, or the degenerations
of capitalism. The study by Loubet del Bayle on
France in the Thirties,[41] on the nonconformists, is
extremely important in this connection. Similarly,

there is a great increase in interest in communism and the Soviet Union; but there is also a great deal of interest in the Italian fascist experience and even in the national socialist experience in Germany. At the height of this interest there are some widespread cultural attitudes, organizations are born, and groups and movements of a prefascist or fascist type emerge and develop all over Europe. There is not a single country that does not have a movement of this type, sometimes limited, sometimes not. Here Nolte is right, but only in a marginal sense. It is a mistake to seek a minimum common denominator more consistent than that which I have outlined.

Ledeen: Does this minimum common denominator exist?

De Felice: The common denominator is this state of mind that is critical of a series of things.

Ledeen: As an ideology, or as a desire to create a certain kind of regime, a certain kind of state?

De Felice: A certain kind of state I would not say. Aside from the fact that it is difficult to speak of movements that then did not take shape as governmental power, it is even more difficult to take the so-called fascist governments under German occupation as part of the general model. The war, the occupation, the progressive ideologization of the war, are such that these regimes—wherever they are constituted (in Hungary, in the France of Vichy, in the Norway of Quisling, and so on)—cannot be taken as an indication of an indigenous fascism. They are the result of a specific moment, the war and the occupation by Germany. All that was original in these movements is so conditioned by the reality of the moment, that it is not possible to take them as points of reference. In short, I do not think that the so-called French fascists of the thirties can be considered— even if sometimes they are the same physical persons—as are the French fascists of the Vichy regime. We are on another terrain, the historical reality is different. But perhaps a comparison is not completely arbitrary: It would be as if to say that the Falange of today, or even the Falange of 1939, 1940, or 1941 is the Falange of José Antonio Primo de Rivera. It seems a bit grotesque.

Ledeen: I agree. However, if this is true, then there are only two fascisms: German national socialism and Italian fascism.

De Felice: They are the only fascisms that arrived in power in circumstances that one could define as normal, on their own merits, through their own capacities, through their own strengths.

Ledeen: However, earlier we said that there are perhaps more differences than points of similarity between Italian fascism and German nazism. If this is true, the discussion of fascism in general becomes very limited. On the one hand we have German nazism and on the other Italian fascism, but we do not have a model that includes both cases, a common denominator for the two regimes or the two countries.

De Felice: I agree. It is not an accident that in recent years the most important contributions to the analysis of fascism have come from the systematic research of students of the single fascism. These contributions have come above all from West Germany,

the United States, and Italy. The most important
scholars in these countries are now in fundamental
agreement that the analysis of fascism is quite different from that conducted in the years that preceded
our generation. These scholars agree that in the
single fascisms, national characteristics were decisive, such as to make an analysis of fascism in general
unproductive. Mosse's studies on the level of
nationalization of the masses are fundamental, and
serve to illustrate and illuminate the fundamental
differences between national socialism and fascism.
However, the common denominator is there, but it is
much less important than is commonly believed, and
it is a negative common denominator, that is, a series
of things that the fascisms refute—in particular Italian fascism and nazism. When one passes to the
positive elements, to the things that fascism wants to
create, to assert, the differences become very strong,
strong enough to force us to use the term *fascist* with
extreme caution, if we wish to understand historically the peculiarities of the various movements, if
we are truly to understand the entire period in its
complexity.

Ledeen: It seems to me that the movements are almost entirely different, especially insofar as their
conception of human nature is concerned. The profound difference between the fascists' and the nazis'
world views are reflected in the different theories of
racism one finds in the two countries. For Mussolini,
race was not a biological concept but a spiritual one.
According to him, there were different spiritual values in the world, and he believed that in specific,
dramatic moments it was possible to speak of "races"
that coexisted with "nations." This was the case for
fascist Italy, where the genius of the Italian race had

made it possible to construct a fascist state. For those citizens who were not transformed, spontaneously fascisticized, a fascist discipline was required. As Mussolini once said to de Begnac,[42] it was possible for him to Arianize the Jews, something that for Hitler was a violation of the laws of nature.

De Felice: Yes, perhaps the greatest heresy that one could commit.

Ledeen: Exactly. This conception of a temporary policy of discrimination—which would have put the recalcitrant Italians on the road of fascism—is extremely interesting, in the sense that it seems to confirm what we said earlier: That the fundamental scope of fascist action was to prepare Italians for the revolution, a revolution constantly projected into the future and whose specific nature remained obscure. This explains also the tremendous effort directed at youth, because if the revolution is projected into the future, the realization of fascist dreams could only be the work of a new generation.

7
Fascism Today

Ledeen: If it is true that the fascist phenomenon is limited to a given historical moment, does this mean that today there is no longer a base, either in Italy or in Europe, for a revival of fascism? Or do you believe that such a base exists?

De Felice: This subject is both very complicated and very simple—very simple because fascism is a historical fact and has to do with a precise period. Therefore, even if there were a new fascism, it would be something quite different. However, this is too simplistic a response; one must consider this question in a more profound context.

At the level of Italian culture today, we find ourselves between two traditions, that of Garruccio[43] and that of Galli.[44] Garruccio denies that in a modern industrial-pluralistic society a phenomenon of the fascist sort is possible. Fascism, according to him, is possible only at a certain moment in the economic and social development of a country. His analysis is not exactly the same as Organski's,[45] but it brings it to mind. Galli does not agree with this point of view:

He maintains that authoritarianisms (and here it is not clear if by authoritarian he means totalitarian, given the clear distinction that must be made between fascist and authoritarian regimes) are possible even in modern industrial societies.

I tend to agree with Galli's analysis. Above all I agree because fascism can appear to many as the satisfaction of a vague need for rationality and functionality that they believe only an authoritarian regime can guarantee. The second reason (of minor importance) consists in the class struggle. However, this analysis is somewhat doubtful, because it might force us to defend theses like technofascism,[46] that have been presented in Italy, but which convince me very little. Even if we admit that a phenomenon of the fascist type can occur in an industrial society, I ask myself: Beyond the label of fascism that we attach to it, does it correspond in any meaningful way to the model of historical fascism?

It has many elements of historical fascism, but lacks its most essential one. It lacks nationalism, which was a crucial element in historical fascism. In the possible neofascist regime, nationalism no longer exists, both because in Europe there is a general crisis of national values (micronationalisms should not deceive us; they are manifestations of this crisis), and because, at the level of the great modern industrial states, nationalism is insufficient to justify a national policy. If we consider present neofascist groups, nationalism has substantially disappeared. In its place there is a kind of Europeanism, which might be viewed as supernationalism: Europe against America and against the Soviet Union, a third entity between the two blocs. This Europeanism is the result of the crisis of national values that followed World War II, but it is also explained by the mystique that the neonazis attributed to the Waffen SS, a "communion of the European struggle" in the final months of World War II. It is a substantially new phenomenon.

Ledeen: Yes, it is a new phenomenon; but is there not a common base between the new fascism and the historical phenomenon? I agree that neonazism is based on the values of the last months of the war, but one might say that historical fascism was based on the values of war as well. Therefore, can we not say that like the fascism and nazism of the first postwar period, neonazism comes from the experience of World War II? And if this is true, is there not a strong link between the two fascisms?

DeFelice: It is possible to argue this similarity, but it is only marginally true. This confuses the issue because for Germany and for Italy the 1914-18 war represented two entirely different things. For Italy, there was the mutilated victory that gives fascism its base. But mutilated or not, it was a victorious war. For Germany it was a defeat. This difference in the historical fascisms (which lies at the very basis of their ideologies) does not exist for neofascism. For neofascism there is only defeat. In Italy—or if you like, in Germany years ago—there was a so-called neofascism or neonazism that was a movement of nostalgia (as it was called at the time), of adult persons who had lived through the nazi and fascist period and identified with it.

For a time this kind of fascism attracted some groups of young people who had not lived through fascism. It attracted them not only for reasons of direct personal interest—the family from which they came or the cultural environment in which they grew up—but also because there was a period in which certain consequences of the war (for example, the question of Trieste for Italy, the Alto Adige, of giving a part of the navy to the Soviet Union) kept nationalistic and patriotic motives alive. Immediately afterward, the cold war permitted the revival of anticommunism of the classic type, which could take a neofascist form.

Aside from these youths, nostalgic neofascism—both in Italy and in Germany—is a phenomenon that is dying out. As far as youth in general is concerned, this kind of neofascism no longer has an effect on them. They still want order and authority and to halt communism, but they tend to participate in movements like the so-called silent majority, which is almost apolitical, or like the MSI-Destra Nazionale, the neofascist party. Here we are dealing with a phenomenon typical of Italy, where politics have taken such a form that a right wing of the classic-traditional sort is unthinkable, because it would immediately be accused of fascism. The Right feels itself to be in such an inferior position psychologically that it would inevitably take on nostalgic connotations. But ideologically it does not count.

Today in Italy there is a phenomenon called *neofascism* (we should eliminate the use of the term *fascism*, at least for historians, because there is such a confusion in this field).[47] There is a serious phenomenon, which I would not call either fascism or neofascism, but simply radicalism of the Right or neonazism, which is quite different from neofascism. If we look at the exponents of radicalism of the Right, the extraparliamentary Right—to use today's terminology—we must ask ourselves: Who are their heroes? What are their models? Is Mussolini one of their heroes—very vaguely, in the same way that Garibaldi is a hero? This statement may sound like a joke, but it is true: All Italians consider Garibaldi a hero. And all those who are opposed to a democratic system consider Mussolini to be a hero. But he is irrelevant. The radicals of the Right do not even extol the Italian fascist experience, because it was a failure; not just because it lost the war, but because Italian fascism failed to create a true fascist state. Their true heroes are others: They are Evola, Codreanu, and the nazis themselves.

These names are extremely important. Who is Evola? It is not an accident that Evola was a marginal figure during the entire fascist period. He never had a role in the fascist party (he was not even a member, at least for a long period of time), he was criticized and viewed suspiciously by many fascists. Evola represents a form of traditionalism, a conception that integrates cosmo-history and catastrophism. These are not found in fascism. At most, they represent extremely marginal components.

The other reference is to Codreanu—Weber is right when he says: Where should we put him? You say that fascism is petite bourgeois, and so on. Well, Codreanu's movement is anything but petite bourgeois; it is a movement of students, of déclassé's, a popular peasant movement—everything, aside from a movement of the middle classes. This observation is true, but Codreanu is not, strictly speaking, a fascist. Codreanu fought against bourgeois values and institutions; these were his continous polemical points of reference, as they are for the radical Right of today, for the present neonazis.

Let us not be deceived by polemical mythology; there is some bourgeois rhetoric in fascism, but it is marginal. The phenomenon has to be viewed in its entirety, in its principal aspects, not in polemical and

transitory ones carried forward under certain circumstances for one tactical reason or another. If we
said that Codreanu fought bourgeois values and institutions, we must also say that fascism was not a
movement that fought bourgeois values and institutions; it wanted to purify them, perfect them; it
wanted to carry forward a point of view, not liquidate
it.

In one of his writings of 1943 (but he had stated it
earlier) Déat maintained that the fascist revolution
was none other than the application of the principles
of 1789.[48] This concept is true in the sense that Talmon has illuminated so well.[49] Fascism involves a
very precise idea of historical progress, and in this
concept the tradition and values of the bourgeoisie
are included in order to be overcome, not denied nor
destroyed. Right-wing radical groups, on the other
hand, completely challenge this line, just as the nazis
challenged it.

I have not been the only one to maintain that fascism is a sort of radicalism in the tradition of radical
parties in Italy—and here I am not referring to a
radicalism of the Right, but always in Talmon's
sense of the term. Cavallotti can be used as a point of
reference in this matter. Augusto Monti[50] made more
than one mention of this point in discussing Gobetti's
Rivoluzione liberale; Belliani[51] did likewise in the
Critica politica, followed by Zuccarini in 1925. Thus,
in the heat of the moment when events were clearer,
this fact did not elude analysts. But later the imposition of various polemics and the transformation of the
regime made these factors seem less evident. The job
of true historians is to bring the original element
back into the light.

There is a beautiful book—the most beautiful that
has been written on that extremely difficult theme of

fascist ideology—by Kunnas,[52] a Fin who, although he only treats the most famous exponents of European fascist culture, has until now seen certain basic ideas more clearly than anyone else. In his analysis there are various points that I am attempting to develop, and, I would like to add, that there is a profound difference between fascism and nazism, and even more between fascism and the neonazism of the present. There are profoundly different aspects of a cultural and ideological type, and others of a psychological and moral type, indicating a clear separation between the two movements that cannot be ignored.

Reading the books written by fascists, looking at fascist propaganda and fascist newspapers, what strikes the observer is a vitalistic optimism that represents joy, youth, life, enthusiasm, and the idea of a struggle for life. This outlook, though framed in fascist terms, is one of progress. In nazism this does not exist. There is no idea of progress; if anything there is one of tradition, of race.

Ledeen: If anything, there is the ideal of regression, of turning back.

De Felice: The very concept of the cycle, which is so strong in nazism, denies the idea of progress. There is optimism in nazism as well, but it is not vitalistic like that of fascism. It is rather a tragic optimism, which in the last period of the war—with the growing conviction that European civilization was condemned to degeneration—transformed itself into its opposite, and was similar to certain kinds of Italian fascism during the Salò period. There is a song of the soldiers of Salò that has been recalled more than once, which goes roughly: "The women don't love us anymore because we wear black shirts," in which one finds (as in other manifestations of the Republic of Salò and of the German Waffen SS in the final days of the war) a strong tragic pessimism, a tragic sense of awaiting death. This outlook characterizes right-wing radicals today, present neonazism, which does not struggle for the future. These people are fighting for a demoniacal affirmation of their own personalities, of their own egos, against everything else. It is an affirmation of supermanism that knows it will die, but that says: "I want you to see that I have the courage to fight against you; even if I stop you only for a decade, only for a year, only for a day, it is an affirmation of my personality against you. But I know perfectly well that I am virtually dead." This factor distinguishes historical fascism from contemporary neonazism, and it indicates not only the enormous difference, but also determines the dramatic powerlessness of these people today. Here we are no longer in the field of political thought but of fanaticism, which is an end in itself.

Ledeen: It is no accident that one of their greatest intellectual heroes who represents a model of this mentality committed suicide, Drieu La Rochelle.

De Felice: I do not know if you agree with this kind of analysis, both insofar as the difference between fascism and nazism is concerned—between vitalistic optimism and the tragic one of national socialism, to the tragic pessimism of right-wing groups today—and in distinguishing, at least from the ideological point of view, these groups from Italian historical fascism.

Ledeen: Yes, I agree. What strikes me about the so-called fascism of today is its almost complete lack of that focus which was such a central idea for fascism itself: the revolutionary element. They talk about everything, of saving the West, the struggle against communism, the struggle against industrial society, but they never speak of revolution.

De Felice: No, because they do not want a revolution, they want the restoration of a tradition. They attempt incredible acts of restoration, incredible even for a fascist logic. They attempt to recover, for example, a certain kind of Christianity, which true fascism, fascism as movement, absolutely never wanted. Fascism as regime made the concordat with the Church, but fascism as movement was anticlerical, and put itself against the most profound values of Christianity. The groups of today are looking for a tradition, which often is not only a mystical one, but magical-mystical as well, which Italian fascism never knew.

Ledeen: However, German national socialism did.

De Felice: This simply provides additional elements for what I said earlier: There is a minimum common denominator, and one finds it in politics, that does not preexist in ideology.

Ledeen: If we can summarize here what we have said about fascism, neofascism, protofascism, and the like, it is clear that you are in fundamental agreement with Talmon's thesis that fascism is not only something that is born with or immediately after the Great War—even if the war is a determinant in the development of fascism—but something that is also tied to a longer tradition in European history. Talmon speaks about totalitarian democracy, a mass,

plebiscitary democracy, born during the period of the
Terror of the French Revolution, which then continued as an element in European left-wing radical-
sim. Excuse me if we come back to this theme, but the
idea that fascism is tied to a tradition of the revolutionary European Left will seem paradoxical to
many Italian readers.

De Felice: It will seem blasphemous.

Ledeen: It will seem blasphemous that fascism has
something in common with the French Revolution,
with a democratic revolution. Will you explain this
paradox?

De Felice: It is not a paradox. Talmon's analysis is
known in Italy by now, even if it has never been taken
as seriously as it should have been. Insofar as Italian
fascism is concerned, I am in complete agreement
with Talmon's analysis; but I do not agree if it were
extended to nazism. I, too, see in fascism a manifestation of that left-wing totalitarianism of which Talmon speaks. Nazism, however, is tied to a right-wing
totalitarianism and should be discussed in terms of a
different analysis, namely Mosse's of nationalization
of the masses. Talmon's analysis is extremely
stimulating, and it is one of the keys in understanding the origins of fascism.

If certain ideological and moral roots of fascism
sprang from the soil of the French Revolution, this
does not mean that the decisive, explosive fact, the
detonator that put the entire process in motion, was
not World War I. I do not believe that without World
War I there would have been fascism, because it is
only that conflict which determined the political, economic, and social conditions without which the

analysis of "roots" would not exist, because there would be no possibility of their taking form. This analysis applies only to fascism as movement, not to fascism as regime. On the contrary, fascism as regime is the progressive imposition on these themes of others of a traditional sort, of totalitarianism of the Right, of Catholicism, and so forth. These are motivations that overpower the entire picture and suggest a reality for fascism that, if it is not examined profoundly and impartially, leads one to erroneous conclusions.

8
Fascism and Totalitarianism; Aspects for Further Research

Ledeen: In an article I wrote several years ago,[53] I spoke about the change in the interpretation of fascism in the historical literature of the last twenty years. I argued that at the end of World War II we had a model of something called *fascism* that in turn was part of a more general phenomenon called *totalitarianism*. In that article I said that this interpretation of fascism was due to the fact that we Americans, English, French, and others had fought against fascism and that during the war, we had created and used the image of the war against fascism in order to mobilize public opinion, to generate propaganda against our enemies.

This wartime concept of fascism as a monolithic unit passed into the literature of history, sociology, and political science. With the passage of time this concept slowly dissolved, and we have arrived at the one of today, which is much more subtle and mature. This process of transformation of the idea of fascism in American and English literature is in great part due to your work. In America in particular, almost all the books published about fascism refer to your research. By now, aside from some reserves here and there (I am thinking, for example, of Stuart Wolff and the seminar he held at Reading a few years ago),[54] we are more or less in agreement with you in distinguishing between fascism and nazism.

However, in Italy your work has been strongly criticized. It has not been received as favorably as elsewhere. How do you explain this situation?

De Felice: This matter is very complicated. I agree with you that in Italy many historians and political writers have strongly attacked my theses, at least when they first appeared. Since then they have created a sort of wall of silence around my analyses and my interpretaions of fascism. This reaction did not happen only for my book; it is true in a more general sense.

For example, the analysis of totalitarianism to which you referred has had very small circulation in Italy. I do not want to shed many tears over this fact because while there are positive elements in the theory of totalitarianism, it concludes by reducing fascism, nazism, and communism (or Stalinism, depending on the author) to a common denominator that I do not accept. It is indicative that this analysis arrived in Italy only with the translation of Hannah Arendt's book,[55] and that for the rest there was silence. Even the work of Friedrich and Brzezinski,[56] to cite an example, has not been translated into Italian. And not only has this book not been translated, but the entire discussion of totalitarianism has also never arrived here. Yet the theory had great success, not only in the United States, but even more so in Germany. In Italy, nothing is known of all this, it has remained an analysis for a handful of specialists who for the most part reject it.

In Italy the discussion of fascism—precisely because we lived it, we felt it with a drama and an
immediacy that certainly did not exist in the United
States, and that the English, even in the most dramatic moments, did not experience, even though they
lived the nazi and fascist periods at first hand—has
been conducted in explicitly political terms and not
infrequently takes its shape from the propaganda of
the war of which you spoke earlier. Consequently, the
models for the analysis of fascism in Italy come from
fascism itself.

All the analyses that have been undertaken for
Germany and for Italy, even though they vary drasti-
cally among themselves, have a common element:
The theory of the great explosion of a collective demon. A dramatic, collective demon, almost Lucifer in
the bottom of Dantë's Hell. In the case of nazism it is a
terrible demon; for Italian fascism, a bit laughable
but always a demon. This kind of interpretation has
had great literary success. There are famous writers
in Italy who have written the priapic history of fascism,[57] which may be entertaining, but which has
very little to do with the reality of fascism. Rather
than helping to understand fascism, this only in-
creases the confusion about it. This fact has been very
important at the level of popular culture, whereas at
the academic level Marxist interpretation has had
the greatest impact. The theory of fascism as class
reaction, as a manifestation of imperialism at a certain phase, with all the modernizations and subtleties of a refined historiography—like the
Italian-Marxist tradition—remains an analysis
closed to every other insight and suggestion. It ends
by burning all the other "classic" interpretations,
certainly the radical one, and if one looks closely, the
liberal one of the "moral disease" as well.

This situation explains why the theory of totalitarianism did not circulate in Italy. This theory meant, with all the possible and imaginable differences, putting fascism, nazism, and Stalinism on the same plane, at least the same moral plane (note here that I do not even say communism, only Stalinism). This reasoning is absolutely unacceptable in a culture like that of Italy, manipulated and determined by the cultural hegemony of the Communist party. This is why the theory of totalitarianism was liquidated in short order.

Even if I do not accept it, this theory warrants discussion because, even if it explains precious little, some elements of its analysis are valid in explaining the functioning of the regime. Instead, it was completely liquidated with the accusation of anticommunism and of being part of the cold war. If someone spoke about it, he heard himself accused of being a camouflaged fascist attempting to propagate fascist theses in scientific garb.

The attitude toward my work has been different. On the one hand, I have suffered a systematic attack, because my analysis does not fit into a Marxist framework, since I do not accept the interpretation that reduces fascism exclusively to class motives and—even while I recognize that these motives existed and are very important—I deny that they are the most important and characteristic. On the other hand, there have been those who wanted to see my work as an attempt to justify the prefascist ruling class and indeed fascism itself, claiming that I presented them in the "best light." In both cases the analysis has been much more political than scientific. There has never been a serious discussion of the problems that are at the basis of my research on fascism. This kind of discussion has been avoided.

Ledeen: How do you explain this?

De Felice: I explain it with an accusation that has been directed at me in various forms: That my analysis of fascism is extremely dangerous politically.

Ledeen: Dangerous in what sense?

De Felice: Dangerous because those people who make this accusation probably think that an analysis like mine might rehabilitate fascism. I am convinced, on the other hand, that if there is one person who emerges fundamentally criticized and in many ways destroyed by my work, that person is Mussolini— destroyed above and beyond his tactical and political capacity, that no one in good faith can challenge. Even Terracini[58] has recently recognized the great political capacity of Mussolini.

My critique is one that functions inside Mussolini, at a more profound level, beyond the noisy phrases and the true and occasionally false accusations that have been directed against him to destroy him summarily, but which in reality destroy nothing. Facts are much more eloquent and persuasive than the panegyrics of an oversimplifed antifascism.

What has irritated many, and in particular those of a certain age, is what has been defined as my objectivity, my serenity in evaluating certain persons, certain events, as if one were talking about events of two or three centuries past.

Ledeen: You are saying that first it is necessary to dig up the facts, reconstruct the history of a certain period, and only afterwards evaluate and judge. Before arriving at the analysis, at the model that explains, one must reconstruct that which is to be explained.

In Italy, on the other hand, if I understand what you are saying, there is an interpretive tradition based on certain presuppositions, certain models, which already "explain" that which has never been reconstructed in its essentials. These presuppositions account for a certain resistance by whoever attempts to carry this work of reconstruction forward.

De Felice: Years ago—when I wrote my first volume, *Il Revoluzionario*, and certainly the first volume of *Il Fascista*, and maybe even when the second had appeared—Ernesto Ragionieri published Togliatti's *Lessons on Fascism*. In these *Lessons*, which I could not have known about when I wrote my books, I found certain of my central themes about fascism. No one, even in passing, noticed this "strange" fact. Aside from the personal aspects, this situation can be explained in two ways: Either with the embarrassment of having to admit the fact, or with the fear of having to open a "premature" or "perilous" discussion that in reality they do not want to undertake, preferring instead a progressive revision of "homemade" judgment and evaluations.

Ledeen: What do you think are the prospects for the future development of Italian historiography on fascism?

De Felice: Italian historiography on fascism has been and will be for a certain period conditioned by the political atmosphere. If the Italian political atmosphere becomes calmer, the historiography of fascism will gain a great deal in objectivity and accuracy. Otherwise, we run the risk of losing further

ground. We shall return to the apodictive claims, the
demonologies, to the interpretations based on a vul-
gar class analysis that does not take any sociological
subtleties into account and that does not attempt to
look at reality. This is a grave danger, and symptoms
of it, eloquent symptoms, are not lacking at the present time.

Even if the fact pleases no one—it does not please
the overwhelming majority of historians and certainly does not please me—fascism was a very important event in the history of Italy and of Europe. Until
we succeed in confronting this great problem in historical terms, we shall not succeed in liberating ourselves from a series of contradictions and incapacities
not only in understanding Italian history, but the
Italian political situation of today as well. That is to
say, in the last analysis, we shall be unable to study
politics seriously.

Ledeen: An American philosopher, George San-
tayana, wrote, "He who does not understand his own
history is destined to repeat it."

De Felice: I do not believe in certain resurrections, in
certain revivals of fascism in terms such as these.
This belief confirms the necessity of undertaking the
study of fascism without preordained models or blin-
ders, to understand and recognize why fascism
existed and to what extent our society is still con-
taminated by it. This necessity is felt by very few
people today. But perhaps there are more than might
appear at first sight. The interest that—at the level of
both sales and journalistic response—the fourth volume of my biography of Mussolini created is perhaps
a symptom that something is moving in this direction, especially among the young and among those

politicians who can see politics not statically, as "patriotism of party" or a desperate defense of all their past ideas and positions, but dynamically, as a continuous acquisition of new elements, as a continuous progress in the understanding of present and past realities. The more and the faster that politics acquires historical consciousness, the more and the faster it can adapt to the new reality and have an effect on it.

Recent attempts to historicize fascism and the Resistance that a politician like Georgio Amendola has felt the need to undertake[59] are symptomatic of the political and cultural situation in Italy. On the one hand, they illustrate—by counterpoint—the abstractnesss and cultural conformism of many of our historians; on the other hand, they offer the possibility of evaluating communist cultural hegemony. From the mouth of a noncommunist, many of Amendola's affirmations would be considered heresies, and the spirit of his analysis would be considered moderate if not downright reactionary, while coming from Amendola they acquire authority and citizenship.

NOTES

1. *Italia giacobina* (Naples, 1965); *La vendita dei beni nazionali nella repubblica romana, 1798-1799* (Rome, 1960); *Note e ricerche surgli "illuminati" e sul misticismo rivoluzionario (1789-1800)* (Rome, 1960); *I giornali giacobini italiani* (ed. Renzo De Felice; Milan, 1962).
2. *Giacobini italiani*, vol. 2 (ed. Delio Cantimori and Renzo De Felice; Bari, 1964).
3. Delio Cantimori, *Conversando di storia* (Bari, 1967).
4. Ibid., pp. 132ff.
5. R. De Felice, "Giovanni Preziosi e le origini del fascismo, 1917-1931," in *Rivista storica del socialismo* (Sept.-Dec. 1962).
6. Benedetto Croce, "L'obiezione contro la 'storia dei propri tempi,'" in *Quaderni della Critica n. 6* (March 1950), pp. 36ff.
7. Reproduced in *Italia giacobina*.
8. In *La rassegna mensile d'Israel*, no. 11 (1956), and no. 2 (1957).
9. R. De Felice, *Storia degli ebrei italiani sotto il fascismo* (Turin, 1962).
10. Angelo Tasca, *Nascita e avvento del fascismo. L'Italia dal 1918 al 1922* (Bari, 1971).
11. George L. Mosse, *The Nationalization of the Masses* (New York, 1975).
12. Johan Huizinga, *The Waning of the Middle Ages* (New York, 1950).
13. Marc Bloch, *Les Rois Thaumaturgues* (Paris, n.d.).
14. For Mosse, the "new politics" is that thread which runs from the French Revolution (and in particular from the Rous-

seauian notion of the "general will") to the "fascist style." This
line of development entailed, in the case of Germany, the evolution of a secular religion, "the cult of the people for itself." The
"new politics," in Mosse's view, made possible the creation of
mass movements at the end of the last century, and created the
necessary soil for the success of the fascist movements of our
century.

15. The "nationalization of the masses," according to Mosse,
was the result of the new politics: the unshaped masses of the
"people" became a mass movement united in its faith in popular
unity.

16. *Rivista storica italiana* 2 (1967):438ff.

17. Luigi Salvatorelli, *Nazionalfascismo* (Turin, 1923).

18. Antonio Cappa, *Due rivoluzioni mancate* (Foligno, 1923).

19. Guido Dorso, *La Rivoluzione meridionale* (Turin, 1925).

20. Cf. Paolo Sylos Labini, *Saggio sulle classi sociali* (Bari,
1975).

21. Cf. Simona Colarizi, *I democratici all'opposizione*
(Bologna, 1973).

22. Cf. *La Carta del Carnaro nei testi di Alceste De Ambris e di
Gabriele D'Annunzio* (ed. R. De Felice; Bologna, 1974).

23. Cf. Michael A. Ledeen, "The War as a Style of Life," in *The
War Generation* (ed. Stephen Ward; New York, 1975).

24. Leon Trotsky, *The Revolution Betrayed* (New York, 1955).

25. From the name of Count Vincenzo Ottorino Gentiloni (cf.
the Glossary of names and historical events).

26. Federico Chabod, *L'Italia contemporanea (1918-1948)* (Turin, 1961).

27. Filippo Buonarotti, *Congiura per l'eguaglianza o di Babeuf*
(Turin, 1946).

28. Irving Louis Horowitz, *Radicalism and the Revolt against
Reason* (Carbondale, 1968).

29. Cf. Michael A. Ledeen, "Fascist Social Policy," in *The Use
and Abuse of Social Science* (ed. I.L. Horowitz; New Brunswick,
1971).

30. Riccardo Korherr, *Regresso delle nascite: morte dei popoli*
(Rome, 1928).

31. Cf. Michael A. Ledeen, *Universal Fascism* (New York,
1972), esp. ch. 1 and 2.

32. One of these analyses by Paolo Farneti, on the crisis of
Italian democracy and fascism's rise to power, will be published
in a forthcoming number of the *Rivista italiana di scienza*

politica. Some previews of Farneti's conclusions about the transformation of the ruling class during the Fascist Regime can be found in Giorgio Galli,*I partiti politici* (Turin, 1974), pp. 253, 268.

33. Palmiro Togliatti, *Lezioni sul fascismo* (Rome, 1970), pp. 97ff.

34. Mosse, ch. 7.

35. Joachim Fest, *Hitler* (London, 1975).

36. Eugen Weber,*Varieties of Fascism* (Princeton, 1964); "The Men of the Archangel," in *International Fascism* (ed. G.L. Mosse and W. Laquer; London and New York, 1969).

37. A. James Gregor, *The Ideology of Fascism* (Berkeley and Los Angeles, 1970); idem, *Interpretations of Fascism* (Morristown, 1974); idem, *The Fascist Persuasion in Radical Politics* (Princeton, 1974).

38. Gino Germani, "Tradizioni politiche e mobilitazione sociale alle origini di un movimento nazional popolare. il peronismo," *Momenti dell' esperienza politica latino-americana* (ed. L. Garruccio; Bologna, 1974).

39. Ernst Nolte,*The Three Faces of Fascism* (New York, 1964).

40. Nolte attempts to find a common denominator for all fascisms. He believes that fascism is born out of an existential crisis of liberal society, challenged by communist revolution. The basis for all fascisms is therefore to be found in the fear of a "leap into the blue," which communism produces in liberal society. It is important to stress, however, that Nolte does not believe that one can equate fascism with anticommunism, even though he does insist that there can be no fascism without an internal communist menace. On the basis of this model, Nolte contends that the period between the two World Wars in Western Europe constitutes a "Fascist Epoch."

41. Jean-Louis Loubet del Bayle,*I non-conformisti degli anni Trenta* (Rome, 1972).

42. Yvon de Begnac, *Palazzo Venezia, storia di un regime* (Rome, 1950), p. 252.

43. Ludovico Garruccio, *L'industrializzazione tra nazionalismo e rivoluzione* (Bologna, 1969).

44. Giorgio Galli, *La crisi italiana e la destra internazionale* (Milan, 1975).

45. A.F. Kenneth Organiski, *Le forme dello sviluppo politico* (Bari, 1970).

46. Cf. Fabrizio Onofri, *Controcultura e rivoluzione* (Rimini, 1974), pp. 137ff.

47. Cf. the suggestion of J. Stuart Woolf, ed., *The Nature of Fascism* (London, 1968).

48. Marcel Déat, *Revolution Francaise et revolution allemande* (Paris, 1943).

49. Jacob L. Talmon, *The Origins of Totalitarian Democracy* (New York, 1951); idem, *Politischer Messianismus*, 2 vols. (Cologne, 1962-63).

50. Augusto Monti, "Nazionalfascismo o radicalfascismo?," in *La Rivoluzione liberale*, 17 July 1923; idem, "Ancora sul radicalfascismo," *La Rivoluzione liberale*, September 1923.

51. Camillo Belliani, "L'Associazione dei Combattenti (Appunti per una storia politica dell'ultimo quinquennio)," in *La critica politica*, 25 July 1924.

52. Tarmo Kunnas, *Drieu La Rochelle, Celine, Brasillach et la tentation fasciste* (Paris, 1972).

53. Michael A. Ledeen, "Fascist Social Policy."

54. J. Stuart Woolf.

55. Hannah Arendt, *The Origins of Totalitarianism* (New York, 1951).

56. Carl Friedrich and Zbigniew Brzezinski, *Totalitarian Dictatorship and Autocracy* (Cambridge, Mass., 1965).

57. Carlo Emilio Gadda, *Eros e Priapo* (Milan, 1967).

58. Umberto Terracini in *Epoca*, 8 February 1975.

59. Giorgio Amendola in *Mondo operaio*, no. 10 (1974), pp. 80-83.

Glossary

Action Francaise.

A French monarchical and ultranationalistic movement (1899-1944), under the leadership of Charles Maurras.

Antonescu, Ion (1882-1946).

Rumanian general. In 1940 he forced King Carol II to abdicate the throne, and assumed all powers as "conducator" of the country. His dictatorship suppressed all other political groups, including the Iron Guard, which had supported him earlier.

Beneduce, Alberto (1877-1944).

Italian financier and politician. In 1912 he organized the *Istituto nazionale di assicurazione*, and became Minister of Labor 1921-22. At first hostile to fascism, he slowly became more favorably inclined toward Mussolini's regime. President of the *Consorzio di credito per le Opere Pubbliche* and of the *Iri*.

Bose, Subhas Chandra (1897-1945).

Originally a member of the extreme left wing of the Indian Congress party, intensely anti-English, Bose decided that Gandi's methods were too slow and founded his own "Forward Block" in 1939. He fled to Europe in 1941, where he supported the Axis during the war.

Bottai, Giuseppe (1895-1959).

Politician, futurist, leading fascist. Minister of Corporations 1929-32 and of Education 1936-43.

Bourghiba Al-Habib (b. 1903).

The leading exponent of Tunisian nationalism for many years, presently president for life of the Tunisian Republic.

Cantimori, Delio (1904-66).

Professor of modern history at the Universities of Pisa, Messina, and Florence. Author of numerous important studies both on the Enlightenment and methodology.

Castle Estense.

The site, in Ferrara, of one of the most important outbursts of squadrist (fascist) violence on 20 December 1920.

Cavallotti, Felice (1842-98).

Journalist and politician. Radical deputy.

Chabod, Federico (1901-60).

Professor of modern history at the Universities of Perugia, Milan, and Rome. From 1947 to his death, directed the *Istituto italiano per gli studi storici* in Naples. Author of numerous extremely important studies in modern and contemporary Italian history, including a fundamental analysis of Italian foreign policy in the late nineteenth century.

Cini, Vittorio (b. 1885).

Industrialist and financier. Minister of Communications in 1943.

Codreanu, Corneliu Zelea (1899-1938).

Founder of the "Legion of the Archangel Michael" in Rumania, from which sprang the Iron Guard. In 1938 arrested and executed by the government of King Carol II.

Crisis of 1931.

A conflict between the Catholic Church and the Fascist Regime over the question of the *Azione cattolica* (the Church's youth organization). The crisis stemmed from Mussolini's desire to eliminate all nonfascist influences on the formation of the young generations.

De Luca, Giuseppe (1898-1962).

Priest, scholar, and editor. Noted in particular for his studies of the history of "piety."

De Stefani, Alberto (1879-1969).

Economist and fascist politician. Minister of Finance 1922-25.

Drieu La Rochelle, Pierre (1893-1945).

French author and collaborator during the Nazi occupation of France. Committed suicide in 1945.

Dumini, Amerigo (1896-1968).

Stormtrooper during the First World War, squadrist in Tuscany, the leader of the group who kidnapped and murdered G. Matteotti in 1924. For this, he was condemned to six years in prison in 1926, and to life imprisonment in 1947. Released from jail in 1953.

Evola, Julius (1898-1974).

Painter and author. Traditionalist, Spenglerian mystic, and spiritualistic racist.

Federzoni, Luigi (1878-1967).

Leading Nationalist journalist and politician, later a leading fascist. Minister of Colonies 1922-24 and 1926-28, Minister of the Interior 1924-26.

Fermi, Enrico (1901-54).

Physicist, professor of theoretical physics at the University of Rome, Nobel Prize for Physics in 1938. Emigrated to the United States following the passage of the racial laws (his wife was Jewish), where he worked with the group that built the atomic bomb.

Gandi, Mohandas (1869-1948).

Apostle of nonviolence, tireless fighter for Indian independence, assassinated by a Hindu fanatic in 1948.

Gentiloni, Vincenzo Ottorino (1865-1916).

President of the *Unione elettorale cattolica*, which, in 1913, on the occasion of the introduction of universal suffrage in Italy, worked out an agreement with Giolitti (the so-called Gentiloni Pact). The agreement was that where there was a threat of socialist electoral successes, the Catholics would vote for moderate liberal candidates who, in turn, promised not to support anti-Catholic legislation.

Giuriati, Giovanni (1876-1970).

President of the irredentist "Trento and Trieste" Association following the First World War, D'Annunzian (served as the first head of D'Annunzio's Cabinet in Fiume), and fascist. Minister of the Liberated Territories 1923, of Public Works 1925-29, and Secretary of the Fascist Party 1930-31.

Grandi, Dino (b. 1895).

Leading fascist from Bologna. Foreign Minister 1929-32, and Ambassador to Great Britain until 1939. The author of the vote of no confidence in the Grand Council of Fascism, which removed Mussolini on 25 July 1943.

Grassini Sarfatti, Margherita (1883-1961).

Writer and art critic, intimate friend of Mussolini. Emigrated to Latin America in the middle of the 1930s, author of the first official biography of Mussolini, *Dux*.

Heimwehren.

Armed Austrian militia that sprang up following the First World War, primarily to defend Austrian claims to territories in Carynthia and Styria, also claimed by Yugoslavia. Increasingly right wing, became a party in 1930. Ruptured in 1932, when a part joined the Nazis. The rest, under the leadership of Prince E.R. Starhemberg, supported the Dolfuss government. Dissolved in 1936 when mandatory military service was reintroduced.

Le Bon, Gustave (1841-1931).

Reactionary and ultramontane French author, wrote the highly influential *Psychologie des folles* (1895).

Leonetti, Alfonso (b. 1895).

Socialist, then communist, active in the *"Ordine Nuovo"* group, director of the *"Lavoratore"* and of *"l'Unità."* Member of the leadership of the Italian Communist party, in 1930 was one of the "group of three" expelled from the party for political disagreements. Increasingly close to Trotsky, was for several years his personal assistant. Joined the Communist party again following the Liberation.

Occupation of the Factories. September 1920.

Chabod has summarized its importance as follows: "Following September, even though the revolutionary impetus was in decline, the strikes continued and there were disorders, outbursts of violence, and Red initiatives. One wondered where it would all end . . . . Fear, therefore, great discontent, and dislocation . . . ."

Osio, Arturo (1890-1968).

Banker. Originally from the *Partito Popolare*, joined fascism in 1925 and became director general of the *Istituto nazionale di credito per la cooperazione*, which he restructured and transformed into the *Banca Nazionale del Lavoro*.

Palace D'Accursio.

In Bologna, the site of bloody encounters between socialists and fascists, 21 November 1920, which signaled the onslaught of the fascist squads.

Pastore, Ottavio (1887-1965).

Socialist, then communist. Director of the Peidmontese edition of *"Avanti!,"* member of the *"Ordine Nuovo"* group, then director of *"l'Unità."* Exile in Russia and France, became a communist senator following the Second World War.

Preziosi, Giovanni (1881-1945).

Priest, who subsequently left the cloth and became a Nationalist journalist and fascist propagandist. The most notorious fascist anti-Semite, was one of those responsible for the "racial politics and policies" of the Republic of Salò.

Primo De Rivera, José Antonio (1903-36).

Leader of the Spanish Falange, executed by the republicans in 1936. Franco exploited his death by transforming the Falange into his own party.

Quisling, Vidkun (1887-1945).

Norwegian politician and collaborator. Became head of the puppet government of Norway in April 1940, and his name became a synonym of "traitor."

Rathenau, Walther (1867-1922).

German industrialist, democrat, and statesman. In the early years of the Weimar Republic was Minister of Reconstruction, then Foreign Minister. Assassinated by ultranationalists.

Rocca, Massimo (1884-1974).

Individualist, anarchist, journalist, and publicist (wrote under the pseudonym Libero Tancredi). Interventionist in the First World War, followed Mussolini, and, in the period immediately following the "March on Rome," led the revisionist and moderate wing of fascism. Expelled from the Fascist party, emigrated to France.

Rocco, Alfredo (1875-1935).

Leading Nationalist and jurist, then fascist. Minister of Justice 1925-32, had a leading role in the organization of the Fascist State.

Rossi, Cesare (1887-1967).

Revolutionary syndicalist, interventionist in the First World War. One of the founders of the fascist movement, Mussolini's closest collaborator until the Matteotti murder. As head of the Press Office of Mussolini, was implicated in the Matteotti affair in 1924, and purged. Fled to France and Switzerland, where he was captured and brought to Italy where he was sentenced to thirty years imprisonment. After the Liberation, conducted an intense journalistic career.

Serpieri, Arrigo (1877-1949).

University professor, expert in agriculture and economics. Closely allied to Nitti (in 1912 he organized the *Istituto superiore forestale* in Florence), he was Undersecretary of Agriculture 1923-24 and of Reclamation 1929-35.

Sorel, Georges (1847-1922).

French revolutionary syndicalist. Author, among other important works, of *Reflections sur la violence* (1908).

Speer, Albert (b. 1905).

Hitler's favorite architect. Minister of Armaments during the Second World War, one of the leading figures in the Third Reich. At Nuremburg, condemned to twenty years' imprisonment at Spandau. Free since 1966.

Starhemberg, Ernst Rudiger (1899-1956).

Austrian political leader. After a brief flirtation with nazism, became leader of the Heimwehren, which he directed in a pro-Italian direction, and opposed the *Anschluss.* During the Second World War, fought in the Free French Air Force.

Turati, Augusto (1888-1955).

Secretary of the Fascist party from 1926 to 1930. Under his direction, the party undertook a vast purge, eliminating many recalcitrant elements.

Waffen SS.

The military wing of the German SS during the Second World War. Since they were not part of the regular Army, their participation in the war was voluntary. They were therefore condemned as criminals (not having the excuse of "following orders") by the Nuremberg Tribunal at the end of the war.

Biography
Bibliography

Renzo De Felice was born in Rieti in 1929. He is presently professor of the history of political parties at the University of Rome. Author of a monumental biography of Mussolini (it presently runs to four massive volumes, over three thousand pages, dealing with the life of the dictator through 1936), he is widely considered to be the world's leading expert on Italian fascism. In addition to his work on Mussolini and several collateral volumes on fascism, he has been instrumental in writing the history of "D'Annunzianism" in the immediate postwar period, publishing the correspondence between D'Annunzio and Mussolini, and between D'Annunzio and Alceste De Ambris.

Selected Bibliography

1962. *Storia degli ebrei italiani sotto il fascismo*. Turin.

1965. *Italia giacobina*. Naples.

1965. *Mussolini il rivoluzionario*. Turin.

1966. *Mussolini il fascista I: la conquista del potere*. Turin.

1966. *Sindicalismo rivoluzionario e fiumanesimo nel carteggio De Ambris-D'Annunzio*. Brescia.

1968. *Mussolini il fascista II: L'organizzazione dello stato fascista*. Turin.

1969. *Le interpretazioni del fascismo*. Bari.

1973. *Carteggio Mussolini-D'Annunzio*. Milan.

1974. *Mussolini il duce I: gli anni del consenso.* Turin.

1974. *La carta del carnaro nei testi di Alceste De Ambris e di Gabriele D'Annunzio.* Bologna.

1975. *La Penultima Ventura.* Milan.

Michael A. Ledeen was born in Los Angeles in 1941. He is presently Senior Fulbright Lecturer at the University of Rome. After receiving his Ph.D. from the University of Wisconsin, he taught for several years at Washington University (St. Louis). He is the author of numerous articles on various aspects of Italian fascism, and is currently preparing a book on the Jews of Fascist Italy.

Selected Bibliography

1969. "Italian Fascism and Youth." *Journal of Contemporary History*, July.

1971. "Fascist Social Policy." In *The Use and Abuse of Social Science.* Edited by Irving Louis Horowitz. New Brunswick.

1972. *Universal Fascism.* New York.

1972. "Fascism and the Generation Gap." *European Studies Review* 1, no. 2.

1975. "The Evolution of Italian Fascist Anti-Semitism." *Jewish Social Studies*, January.

1975. *D'Annunzio a Fiume.* Bari and Rome.

1975. "The War as a Style of Life." In *The War Generation.* Edited by S. Ward. New York.